Coaching, Training & Developing The Retail Manager

Retail Consulting Skills For Store Managers

Richard Bell, MSM

Copyright © 2013 Richard Bell

All rights reserved.

ISBN: 10:1492188670
ISBN-13: 978-1492188674

Cover Photo: © Skypixel | Dreamstime.com

DEDICATION

This book is dedicated to my son, Noah. You are the inspiration in everything I achieve.

CONTENTS

1	The Retail Consultant	1
2	The Retail Consultant in Every Store Manager	12
3	Business Identifiers	32
4	The Retail Consulting Principles	49
5	Training Wheels	69
6	Undercurrents in the Environment	116
7	The Broken Building Environment	136
8	Customer Engagement	162
9	Competitive Diagnosis	178
10	Planning for Success	193

OTHER TITLES AVAILABLE

Coaching Training & Developing The Retail Manager

Coaching, Training & Developing The Retail Manager: The Retail Leadership Bridge

Chapter 1

THE RETAIL CONSULTANT

A retail environment is a complex and diverse universe. It has many moving parts with a blend of personalities and work ethics. This diverse world presents many positive experiences as well as challenges. The experience and skill-set of a manager to sort through and implement solutions remain the largest challenge.

The search for resolutions requires a universal view of the business and people. There are many variables to consider when making decisions. The decisions will influence customer service and results. A disregard for the internal and external influences on the retail store will provide short-term results and fail to make a long-term impression.

The failure in creating and implementing solutions is twofold.

Managers, in many instances, lack understanding of the elements that influence their store. Managers are not coached, trained and developed to recognize influences or barriers to problem solving. They make decisions based upon experiences and achieving an immediate fix.

Managers must learn to view their world as a whole system and from a consultative point of view. A consultative perspective views the retail world through an understanding of the problem, the world that surrounds the problem, contributors to a problem and alternate solutions for solving a problem. It is a discipline and requires managerial maturity to reveal the many issues beneath the surface of an environment that influence outcomes.

Coaching, Training & Developing The Retail Manager: Retail Consulting Skills For Store Managers will take a look at common problems that plague the retail store environment today. The issues include developmental opportunities in people, processes and presentation. The people component includes both customers and employees. The solutions require both time and commitment to work. The problems were not created overnight and cannot be fixed overnight with lasting results. Your role is to keep an open mind and consider the value of alternate solutions. Your role is also viewing problem solving through a leadership lens that presents a healthier environment today than before the problems were discovered.

Putting Out Fires

Retail managers spend a large part of their day putting out fires. They chase problems and apply quick, immediate solutions. The solutions do not typically consider the whole system or surrounding areas that may be impacted. The solution, in essence, may create additional problems down the road or may not resolve the underlying issues of the problem.

This approach to solving problems finds a manager chasing their tail to get things accomplished. There is never much thought or consideration for the long-term impact of decisions on the store or achievement of goals. The rushed spirit of decision-making in the store is disguised as the necessity to get everything done in a day.

The plan for most days is altered by the fluctuations of customer business and complaints, employee call-offs, progress of projects, competitive influences, weather and corporate visits to name a few. These fluctuations cause the most well-planned manager to create immediate short-term solutions to problems. The solution may fix the surface problem but may create issues that arise in other areas.

This method of addressing problems perpetuates itself as one manager passes along this secret of handling the daily operations of the store to another. It is a race to snuff out the problems that interrupt the flow of the day. This method may work for small, immediate decisions such as moving cashiers around to cover busy times or areas. This approach is not effective for strategizing long-term change or during the decision-making process.

Putting out fires will always be a part of the managerial daily routine. In retail, unexpected problems and surprises will always arise. Managers need to be nimble while making decisions that address immediate concerns. This approach will never mesh well with long-term strategies or diagnosing problems that exist. Diagnosis of problems such as a department that has declined in sales will only yield an actionable plan and identification of barriers if all elements are considered. Using a fire mentality during diagnosis will not provide a viable strategy for recovery.

The Retail Consultant

Before we dive into the elements that influence decisions and solutions, we need to look at the composition of a consultative view. There are two terms that are used interchangeably in relation to offering managers guidance and decision making clarity. The terms are consulting and coaching. Though these terms are thought of as the same, they offer a very different approach to business.

A consultant is a professional trained to collect data, observe established norms and behaviors as well as examine contributing factors below the surface in regards to problems and dysfunctional environments. They take an extensive look at the problem and the universe that surrounds the issue and they offer solutions to fix the problem. The solutions are long-term fixes that require managers to implement and support the initiative to achieve successful change. This does not mean the solutions are necessarily easy or convenient. The solutions can be involved or complex or be simple remedies, but they require a buy-in from the Store Manager to see fruition.

Consultants take the problem and ask, *"What does this really mean?"* Not what it appears to be, what does it mean to the environment and how did the problem get there. How does the problem influence the environment negatively? What does the problem contribute to and what is contributing to the problem? A Store Manager, in comparison, will ask, *"How do I fix this problem now?"* The Store Manager is not worried about contributing factors, rather, quickly dissolving the problem and moving forward.

A consultant offers solutions that can be accepted or rejected by the client. They leverage their experience to devise a plan to repair the problem. The repair or solution is ongoing. They provide knowledge and tools for the manager to use to prevent future issues or repair them. They leave behind a usable solution to broaden the abilities of a manager.

External Consultant

The benefits of a consultant can be far reaching. There are two types of consultants. One that is not employed by the company or external and one that is internal. They both have advantages and disadvantages. More companies today are hiring internal consultants to examine the business from various facets such as operational, supply chain or sales diagnostics.

The advantage of an external consultant is looking at a problem from an outside perspective. The external consultant is not entrenched in the established norms of the store. The environment does not influence them. They view productivity through a detached lens. They have distance from the problem and are not involved with any emotions tied to a situation.

For example, an external consultant may be reviewing costs associated with assembling bicycles in a retailer. They are viewing the process from many angles. Jim may be the best bike assembler in the company from a numerical perspective but may also have the most bicycles returned. The consultant is not influenced by Jim's character or personal connections in the environment as the friendliest employee. They are not swayed by good intentions or the fact that Jim has a long history of assembling products. They are examining the process and contributors to the problem. They are not attached to Jim as an internal consultant may be.

The disadvantages of an external consultant consist of the learning curve and lack of understanding nuances that exist in the environment. The nuances contribute to the success or failure of a situation. It will take time to understand established norms that influence the environment. There will also need to be time invested into how people and departments connect that comprise the whole system.

Internal Consultant

The internal consultant can reduce the learning curve by an established understanding of the environment. The internal consultant can foresee barriers and logistical opportunities that may arise. They can get to the heart of the matter in a faster time frame. They also have connections in the company that may be able to improve or expedite material or financial needs.

There are disadvantages to internal consulting. It is difficult for an individual that is close to a situation and the people to remain objective. They are attached to the company, its people and procedures. It is difficult to flip the switch and ignore close relationships. There is an understanding of difficulties that exist in enacting change within the organization that may influence proposed solutions.

The internal consultant can shave considerable time from the discovery phase of the process. The question that remains is can this person step back and look at the situation through an unbiased lens. Take the bicycle assembler example mentioned earlier. If the internal consultant knew Jim and has a close relationship with him and his family, would they be able to make recommendations that may eliminate or change the position? If they are influenced by the relationship, they may not make the best decision or recommend the most efficient solution.

Organizations that have internal consultants feel there is a separation of consultant and front line activity by positioning the individual(s) at the home office. This does allow for some separation, but the individual must be committed to an objective view of a situation. They cannot let the environment along with internal pressures influence their decisions for the store, company and surroundings. A consultant may or may not understand the established norms of the staff that influences behavior and results. The consultant may already have a high-level view of policies and procedures that could potentially influence decision-making.

An example would be evaluating the cost and profit ratio of selling roller skating accessories in a sporting goods store. All indicators may point to a loss in this line with a potential exit of this merchandise. The problem may be the three employees that handle that line may be out of a job, and the consultant goes to lunch with them every day. Would this influence the decision?

Coach

A business coach is a different approach. It is a disciplined approach that involves an outside coach as a guide. They do not offer the answers or solutions that the consultant does. Instead, they ask questions that allow the manager to come up with their own solutions. They do not influence the decision or challenge the proposed solution. This is extremely challenging for most individuals that want to give their opinion and be involved in generating solutions.

There are many different types of coaches available from business to life coaches, but they operate a similar way. They do not say, *"Here is the solution for you,"* rather they ask unbiased questions that stimulate thoughts for the manager. This is tricky as the coach is fighting the desire to interject or speak up when they think the manager is making a bad choice. The coach should not influence the manager's decision.

There are many benefits to coaching. It allows the individual to create possible solutions and think them through to choose the most effective path. It helps the manager remove bias from their decision-making and gives them a conduit to express their thoughts without judgment. The manager applies reflection and forward thinking to evaluate options.

Both consulting and coaching are effective problem solving methods. This book will review problem solving, through a consultative lens, to instill objectivity and whole system thinking to situations. Coaching requires an individual to be a neutral sounding board that may not be available to some managers.

The Consultative Path

The assumption for this book, you are a Store Manager within a retail store or a desire to be in a position of authority. The assumption is necessary to create change in the retail environment. It requires a manager with the authority to implement change. Regardless of a Store Managers current skill-set or level of experience, the method to arrive at long-term decisions probably does not include an analysis of the situation. A manager may be going purely on instinct, reflection of past decisions or influential practices of their managerial mentors.

The advantages and disadvantages of an internal consultant have been explained. Your role in the store as a part of the managerial team aligns with the role of an internal consultant. You already have first-hand knowledge of the store, company and surroundings. You may or may not understand the established norms of the staff that influences behavior and results. As a Store Manager, you may already have a high-level view of policies and procedures that could potentially influence decision-making.

Store Managers may not have the education or training of a consultant. A consultant possesses many disciplines that allow them to view a situation objectively. The objective of this book is not to instantly grant a manager consulting power. It takes many years to establish a grasp of disciplines and processes of consulting. The intent is presenting a more disciplined approach to determining the cause of a situation based on common consulting principles.

The goal is diagnosing a problem that exists within the store, discovering the contributors to the problem, considering the impact of the problem on the whole system and creating solutions. This method is not a quick bandage for a problem, rather, a methodical approach that offers insight into the many variables that comprise the retail environment. The disciplines take considerable time to integrate into the problem solving process.

Unless your organization has an internal consultant that can work with independent units, it is unlikely that managers will be able to enlist the support and expertise of consulting. Left with a choice of limited or no access to consulting, managers must seize the opportunity to learn disciplines to assist the store staff to create and face resolutions to problems.

CHAPTER 2

THE RETAIL CONSULTANT IN EVERY STORE MANAGER

The bad news, even though consultants can provide a vital service to any retail store it is highly unlikely your company will provide one. The good news through discipline and practice you can sharpen your skills to view the environment through a consultative lens. A consultant can view your world objectively because they are not emotionally or financially connected to the store. There are no egos or avoidance of failure to handle. They look at the business and influences on the success or failure of the concentrated area. They provide an in-depth analysis that goes beneath the surface to the actual cause or trigger of an issue. Only after they have discovered what makes the problem tick, they begin to dismantle it through problem solving.

A Retail Consultant can only make recommendations and provide solutions. The solution will only be successful if the Store Manager buys into change and leads the initiative. Many consulting relationships require a mutual resolution created by the consultant and Store Manager. This relationship grants an equal balance of power to both parties to resolve the issues.

If you could learn to view the business like a new store assignment, you can utilize retail-consulting techniques to analyze the store. It is neither simple nor quick to strengthen these elements within you. A Retail Consultant gets to be good at what they do through practice, situational application and mentors. A Store Manager can improve their skills through adopting the techniques, using them in the business and teaching them to Assistant Managers.

The teaching aspect reinforces what a manager is learning as they evolve. The educational role allows for dialogue of potential barriers and contributions to the solution process. The culmination of using, applying and teaching the consulting aspects in all areas of the store is a well-balanced staff at solving problems. You can truly be the consulting voice of the store. The solutions will be based on thorough research and the solutions will be for the long-term.

Influential elements

There are factors that influence the decision making process. The knowledge gained by understanding the power of these internal and external contributors to decision-making and change help to form a more holistic solution. The elements consist of:

- **Bias**
- **Controlling Emotions**
- **Understanding Norms**
- **Whole System View**
- **Who or What Determines Success**

These elements must be considered because they affect the way a manager views situations and create solutions. A manager may consider their demeanor as highly professional, but it is difficult to look at the business objectively. Managers will often take criticism of their daily operation as a personal attack on their leadership skills.

Opportunities will usually arise once they reach the surface. The opportunities are usually reflected in reporting. For example, a product group that is showing a sales decline or department in the store that has taken a sales or margin hit. We do not recognize them as opportunities until we realize the trend is not reversing. Even though the problem has been slowly developing, it is not on the radar until it becomes glaringly obvious. We notice the iceberg on the surface but not the slow build from the bottom-up.

Once the problem presents itself there are many ways a solution can be created and implemented. The far too common way of handling this situation is demanding it be fixed. A Store Manager may throw terms at the team like *"Turn this ship around"* as a form of coaching and feel good about handling the situation. Immediate resolutions are only suitable for short-term situations. They are like a bandage in every way. They are put on the problem, hope it sticks, but it will eventually fall off and may reveal a worsening situation.

A manager is so busy putting out fires that problem solving is reduced to a two-minute consideration. You may not realize that the problem will continue to crop up in other ways and other places. A staffing problem in one department may be fixed by moving a sales person from another area. This will cause one of the other plates you are spinning to fall. It is a balancing act to handle the daily necessities and the barrage of changes influenced by customers, competition and internal demands.

Responding to the elements requires a look past your ego and thought process that problems could not possibly exist within your store. An ego is necessary for Store Managers and Assistants within the store. It creates a desire to be the best and passion to succeed. The downside of an ego is the lack of clarity it offers to identifying problems within the store. An ego can get in the way of progress and development.

Bias

Bias is much like ego in that it makes it difficult to realize opportunities within the store. Bias is showing partiality towards your store or variables within your store. A Store Manager is not viewing reality through a clear lens. Bias can be applied to the performance of your employees and management staff, store performance metrics and even the appearance of the store. The desire to be the best interferes with your ability to see and feel changes in the environment.

Removing your bias for the success of your store and people is not in question. What is in question is removing the blinders or bias to reveal the actual picture. You must learn to view the store and its people objectively. When you view the performance of the store in direct correlation with your ability to lead, you may tend to find any flaws in the store as a personal failure. An investment in coaching, training and developing the staff is in direct correlation with the success of the store. The faults are only a personal failure if you disregard the indicators of a problem and do not take action.

Put aside your personal feelings for the store and its contribution to your personal success. This is easy to say but hard to do when emotions are involved. Take out your emotion by following a path of questions intended to get to the heart of the issue. If a manager applies biased thought to a problem, they may not be able to see the contributors to the situation. The following list of questions is a way to remove your personal investment in the situation and treat it objectively. The time to be personally invested is not at this stage of a process. The opportunity to invest in a personal way is during the implementation and drive for success.

Here is an example of questions that will help to remove your bias and ego from the situation.

- **What is the problem?**
- **What reasons may there be for the problem?**
- **What are the contributors to the problem?**
- **What are/were the indicators that a problem was developing?**
- **How does the problem affect the store?**
- **What level of success could be achieved if the problem is resolved?**
- **Who are the key players in implementing a solution?**

The questions should be designed as a factual hunt for answers. Notice, there are no questions that ask how the Store Manager contributed to the problem. These types of questions, though valid, would create a defensive reaction. The assumption is that managers have contributed to the situation. The significant issue is creating long lasting resolutions.

The road to moving away from bias is like a map. The questions connect to form a path to understanding the situation from a consultative view. Follow the path to view your business as a business without the family feeling attached to it. This is not about what you have done wrong as much as it is what you can do to strengthen the situation for the long-term.

Controlling Emotions

Another tough subject that will influence your decision-making and solutions is your emotions. Your emotions are affected from three perspectives; ego, work invested and connections with people. These perspectives are especially true for managers in a store for many years. In any case, there becomes an attachment between you and the environment. The attachment may interfere with the ability of the manager to make rational decisions.

Controlling Emotions/ Ego

We have already mentioned managers and their egos a little earlier. Having an ego is not necessarily a bad thing. Most managers need to have an ego to want to be the best for the company. At times, the desire to be the best crosses the line to a manager thinking their ideas and actions are always the best. The book Coaching, Training & Developing The Retail Manager explores the problem with wanting to be the smartest person in the store. It is a flawed concept that creates a closed environment for ideas and improvement. A Store Manager needs to be surrounded by the brightest and the best talent. The goal is to assemble a high-performance team.

Ego can at times, become arrogance. This is what clouds the lens of reality. When a manager believes their ability is in-sync with the environment, they may believe major problems simply cannot exist. They do not see the problem as it is forming. The environment is closed so your people do not express concern for compounding issues. Arrogance has become a barrier to surface problems and there is no chance at evaluating underlying concerns.

A consultant does not have the ego associated with running the store. A Store Manager needs to leave their ego at the door when analyzing the environment. You will not acknowledge or recognize the scope of a problem if you do not lose the ego. There is a need to examine the origins of a problem to fix it and that may bring about your culpability in creating the issue. You also need to realize that part of fixing the problem may involve changing the way you manage and lead people.

Here are a few items to consider when thinking about ego:

- **Problem solving requires self-analysis to determine the origins of the issue.**
- **An ego is great for competitive purposes but has no place in identifying problems and creating solutions.**
- **Ego is an emotion that will interfere with the success of constructively solving problems.**
- **A consultative view of your environment requires control of your emotions.**

Remember this process is not about questioning your passion for the store or company. It is not about questioning your desire to be the best for your team and your own career. It is about regulating your emotions and applying emotion when needed. If you are celebrating a big win, be loud and appreciative. Put away your emotions when analyzing your business. There are opportunities for you to catch a problem before it becomes one. When a problem does surface, and they will arise, you will be much better able to diagnose the cause and provide solutions.

Controlling Emotions/ Work-Invested

The work-invested part of controlling your emotions is derived from the sense of accomplishment and sweat put into your store. Store Managers work hard to succeed and overcome obstacles. You have many hours invested beyond the call of duty, which increases the attachment to the store. It represents your sweat equity and contributes to your ego.

Your time and energy invested into the store or job may represent the level of success that your store has today. The reason consultants can see more clearly is they are not invested or attached to the store. They have no sweat equity and are unaware of the time and energy invested into the environment. They see things for what they are, a problem that requires a solution. The problem not only needs a solution, but a long-term fix to keep the situation from reoccurring or showing up somewhere else.

The hard part is letting go of your investment in the store to analyze problems. It is challenging. That is why managers that should have retired years ago hang on to the job. They have their lives invested in the job and find it hard to leave all of that energy behind. This sense of pride has its place but will cloud your judgment at times.

Controlling your emotions is taking a step back from the big picture. It is separating your feelings about the business from the business model itself. Regardless of effort and sacrifices made for the business, you cannot see through them clearly. A Store Manager should take a step back and look at the issues as a business.

Store Managers that have managed various stores analyze the

business for strengths and weaknesses and begin formulating plans. They are not attached or emotional about people or processes. The manager views the business with a need to stabilize areas that need to be shored up and repaired. Look at your store for the first time through these eyes. The business case study follows in Chapters 5 as an example to put your business on paper and examine it like a new assignment. For consultants, every assignment is a new view of different problems.

Controlling Emotions/ Connections with People

One of the most crucial components of any store is its people. My previous books dedicated many pages to the understanding and appreciation of people. For any retail store to be successful, the environment must be conducive to developing people in their roles. The managers must connect with the team to understand their needs. Connecting also motivates the team and removes the barriers that stand in the way of success.

The environment in most stores becomes a family-like atmosphere. People begin to share experiences and rely on each other to complete tasks and work towards a common goal. This sense of a family unit within the store can easily alter your judgment. For example, payroll has been cut, and managers are looking for possible positions to reduce or eliminate. You may come across a position that is expendable, but there is general knowledge about

Sara and her dependency on the job. She may be struggling to make ends meet and taking care of her grandchildren. You may be influenced to eliminate another position because of the first-hand knowledge of the person, not the position.

A consultant does not typically know the person behind the position. They are looking at the staffing picture in terms of value that exists within the position. They are not influenced by the needs of the individual in the job. Having a connection with people is great when running the day-to-day operations of the store but it is a much different scenario when analyzing the business model.

There are smart decisions to make when considering the people element. Aligning people in positions to maximize effectiveness is smart business. There could be a problem in your store with misaligned talent. It could be resolved by making changes for a better fit of talent and position requirements.

Another factor to include with people is a social one. Store Managers cannot make solid business decision about the store and staff if they have a friendship with them. Socializing confuses the role between manager and employee. It may cause you to overlook performance issues. It can also influence your business analysis in the same way as the family scenario. You may be reluctant to alter or eliminate a position if your friend has the job.

It is difficult to remove emotions from your decision-making with people. This scenario is another situation that requires an emotional distance. Look at your business model in positions, not names. Take the people and the personalities out of the job to view the system objectively. You may feel guilty about not focusing on the person in the role. Remember, this is a business analysis that requires a separation from emotion.

Understanding Norms

Norms are the established behaviors that your team exhibits daily. It is the environment created through collaboration and combined efforts of employees. Some norms contribute positively to the environment while others are more destructive in nature. Norms are allowed to develop in the workplace by managers. Directly or indirectly, a manager has either agreed or looked the other way while these habits were forming.

Norms are typically created after a team gets comfortable with their roles and traits of their supervisors. For example, there may be members of the team that always go on break together. It may impact business on the sales floor, but managers have allowed it for months and it has become the expectation.

There are also good norms established by the team in the form of teamwork. They may decide as a group to help with the various tasks that need to be completed daily. There may be an agreement between departments to assist each other during an influx of business. These norms show support, but they may sacrifice customer service in departments.

A Store Manager needs to understand norms that exist in the workplace to gain insight into the way employees perform their jobs. Norms that are allowed to exist become part of the culture and the way employees function. In some cases, it may not be a failure in a process, rather, an established norm that has been permitted to influence results. For example, there may be a process that requires out of stock merchandise be scanned and entered into the system. The team may decide this process does not need to be completed in the crafts section of the store every day. They may scan the area every other day, as opposed to the daily directive. This would need to be considered when evaluating possible issues with the process or in this area of the store.

This example could work in the opposite fashion. The area was supposed to be scanned every other day. A manager may have directed the team to scan the area daily. It may increase sales in the area, or it may account for the team falling behind on other tasks. The point is, norms become an established part of the environment. Norms can influence the current results and can continue to influence results beyond change. If a manager creates change without considering and adjusting norms, the situation may end up with the same results no matter how hard managers try.

Whole System View

Consultants look beyond the impact of a problem or change initiative on one area. They look at the entire model. They understand the pieces and segments of the retail business as the composition of the whole system. The whole system includes everything that influences or will be influenced by a decision or change. This goes beyond the four walls of the store to external influences, as well.

The whole system is comprised of customers, employees, resources, expenses, policies, areas that surround the problem or interest, competition, as well as merchandising and brands. These factors may not be all inclusive and other elements within the whole system may exist to apply to your situation or store. Think in terms of what is impacted by the decisions. Do not think about the environment in a limited short-term view. Long-term development and stability are the goal. The whole system must be considered to make change stick.

Every problem, department, concern or interest, is connected to another element. A change in one department may affect customers, other departments, employees, etc. This is the whole system view. The immediate decision may have long-term repercussions. The changes you apply to a small problem may create other issues in the system.

The consultative view connects the immediate situation to all other elements that may be impacted. How does this problem affect customers? How will the resolution affect customers and employees? How will the long-term change benefit customers, develop employees and challenge the competition? This line of questioning continues to take the original analysis further. It connects the issue and exposes it to the other elements.

When diagnosing a problem, connecting the elements defines the scope of the problem. Just like the iceberg mentioned earlier, the problem is above the surface and visible to the naked eye. The connections exist beneath the surface, the largest part of the iceberg. In retail, this part of the problem has formed over time until it became visible. The whole system has influenced the size and shape of the problem. Store Managers need to see beneath the water to gain insight into the breadth and depth of the problem.

A surprising factor to some is the inclusion of competition in the elements of the whole system. Competitive influences should be considered during diagnosis of a problem. Is the competition offering a product or service that gives them an advantage over your store? A competitor's promotional or local efforts should be evaluated when seeking an explanation for a decline in an area.

Competition should be a factor in planning and creating solutions. You cannot create plans for change with a disregard for the competition. The changes may drive customers to the competition. Competition is under the umbrella of the whole system. They are a part of the external environment that has an influence on results.

Who or What Determines Success

How do you know if solutions will be a success? Who or what determines the success of an implementation or strategy? These questions are not as easy to answer, as they may seem. Too often, a manager creates a plan and implements it. The manager alone determines if the plan is successfully integrated into the environment. This situation presents a difficult evaluation of success. If a manager created the initiative, and it was on their own or in partnership, there is a biased tendency for it to succeed. You may see success even though facts do not support it because you want the initiative to succeed.

A better way to determine success is to have opposing views agree to the overall success of the initiative. For example, there are a few managers and employees from across the store involved with implementation. Some will see the value in the plan while others will oppose the idea. This is the ideal collection of people to determine success. Managers develop implementation plans. Milestones and regularly scheduled meetings should evaluate progress. It is at this point that opposing views discuss the strengths and opportunities of the implementation. Adjustments can be made to ensure implementation is on track or to get it back on track. When the two sides agree that the method has been successfully integrated into the environment, there is a greater chance of this being reality.

There may not always be time or resources for opposing views to determine the actual success of an initiative. Looking through a consultative lens requires thorough analysis and effective, efficient solutions. Part of developing a solution is scheduling a time line and defining specific results. You must also measure the ongoing integration of the initiative. The time line, result specifications, and measures are non-negotiable. Without these absolutes in place, there is no real way of knowing the level of integration, necessary adjustments, resistance and acceptance.

The rules need to be spelled-out before implementation. Thorough diagnosis followed by rushed implementation will not yield long-term results. Managers need to determine the parameters of success by avoiding influential pitfalls. The pitfalls as described in this book consist of controlling your emotions through temperament of biased feelings, ego, sweat equity, connections with people, understanding norms and sharing a whole system view.

Success is determined by the goals and measures met for

consultants. Consultants are not often around to see the outcome. They have two goals with the first providing a comprehensive analysis and solutions for the problem. The second is leaving behind tools in the form of knowledge and approach for managers to use to help themselves going forward. They are providing the framework and a map to follow to achieve results.

Step Back

The design of the influential elements is to keep the focus on the facts. If you focus on the facts, you will less likely be emotionally connected to the information. The facts will also help to present a solution based on actual performance and contributors without a skewed view that includes emotion.

Trying to leave emotions out is tough to do. For this reason, companies hire consultants that are not attached to the business. The advantage that managers have is an intimate knowledge of the store and market. Managers can get to a solution with an understanding of all of the nuances that exist within the environment. An external consultant may never have exposure to all of the variables that exist. They have no emotional investment but there is a longer learning curve in company policies and established norms.

Store Managers have an advantage with diagnosing problems and providing solutions. Managers need to step back and view their world with a factual lens. You need to be further from the emotional investment. The further from emotions, the clearer the problem, will become. This is not a directive to disconnect with people and view your daily business from a distance. This is an investment in understanding the influential elements. This is for the sake of accurate diagnosis of problems and implementing solutions.

CHAPTER 3

BUSINESS IDENTIFIERS

Looking back on the last chapter, there is a lot of information and a lot that influence a store. There are several elements that need to be considered before you begin to "fix" things. The goal is not to put a bandage on the problem, rather, get to the heart of the matter. You must have a handle on the following two questions:

1. **How is the problem influencing the components of the business?**
2. **How are the components of the business creating the problem?**

These two questions are linked together. It cannot just be one way or the other. If you think of a problem as a one way street, you may be missing a key piece to developing a solution. We tend to believe that a problem was created overnight, and it now impacts the business negatively. This is usually brought to light through a declining business segment. We look at a report and understand that a problem exists and is placing a strain on a certain aspect of the business. We immediately try to focus on a singular cause to simplify a solution. It is easy to think that the actions of a singular process or the lack of talent or training of an individual created the problem. In reality, problems are much more complicated.

Understand Your Business Identifiers

Six main drivers comprise the picture or state of the business. These business components are universal regardless of a large or independently run store. Much like a lookout on the Titanic. Store Managers must be in touch with the elements to see or sense a problem rising. Once a ship has hit the iceberg, there is damage done to the ship. Not every problem is life threatening to the business, but the small issues create distractions.

The six main identifiers that contribute to your understanding of a store:

1. **Business Performance (Numerical Data)**
2. **Customers**
3. **Employees/ Environment**
4. **Presentation/ Assortment**
5. **Competition**

6. Processes

There are many other elements that could be added to the list. It is difficult to consider a list of twenty or thirty elements when identifying a problem. Store Managers can use other business metrics to investigate a problem, but the six elements can often lend insight into a problem or potential issue.

The identifiers can also be used as a general observation tool. They can strengthen well performing areas. There may not be a problem, but you should have a handle on the six main identifiers as a way to improve business. There may be a segment that performs well in the store. If you give the segment a quick analysis with the six identifiers, you may find opportunities to strengthen the performance.

The identifiers should be used together. Store Managers cannot dig deep into the core of a problem by just understanding the numbers or the environment. A solid understanding of the six identifiers will immerse you in the environment of the store to see problems at a potential level. If you are basing decisions on one identifier, you may not be making the most educated or productive decision.

Business Performance (Numerical Data)

Major retailers have an endless amount of reporting. The reports are required to measure the success or failure of the business. Most Store Managers understand hard data about their store. They live by the reports generated daily and in most cases manage by the reports. This can be tricky because problems are not recognized until they become a problem. In other words, they will not see the problem coming.

Reporting is an absolute necessity in retail. The only comparative tool that a Store Manager may have is the numerical data available. You need to understand the part of story the numbers represent. The numbers are indicators of something, but they do not tell the whole story. You cannot see an area of decline and immediately understand what is driving the decline. Too often, a Store Manager recognizes an opportunity and issues a demand to get the problem fixed. This will never work and will only result in hiding the problem to continue or return later.

The numbers are an essential part of the story, but they represent the end of the story. Everything has already occurred to drive the number on the page. If you are number centric in your management style, you will not be tapped in to the culture and environment, competition, processes, customers, product assortment or inventory levels of your store. These areas may be contributing or creating the problem. The same goes if you are a people person but avoid the numerical data, you will not have the complete picture.

Learn to see the numerical data as a part of a group of indicators for the health of your store. Reports should be used in conjunction with the other indicators. The reports and indicators determine resolutions to problems. Further reporting or investigation may be required, but the six indicators will help to recognize a situation to be addressed.

Customers

If you were at a retail meeting right now, you would probably list the customer as the most valuable part of the business. Too often for managers, it is lip service and not a real consideration as an identifier of the success or failure of the business. Many Store Managers base their understanding of customers on their understanding of the numerical data. They see a poor performing area and assume this offers insight into what a customer wants or does not want. You may be overlooking factors that influence the poor performance such as employee training, assortment or broken processes.

Customers have the final say on everything. They will tell you what works in the store and what is failing. It is true that consumers are more educated now than ever. They have many additional means to make buying decisions. The Internet and visibility of retailer inventories and pricing present a much more competitive market. Customers can shop competitors from your store on their phone. How important is listening to the customer, with all of the available means that reach customers it is more important today than just ten years ago.

If you are purely number centric, you will never understand the customer. You cannot base buying habits and trends solely on the numbers. You need to know what the customer wants. This can happen in three ways. The first is knowledge of the customer directly. This may be challenging in a large building. If a portion of the customer base is large volume buyers, it may be easier to gain insight into buying habits. Large, frequent trip retail destinations will gain insight through a managerial presence on the sales floor, being immersed with employees in the environment and reporting. The second way to gain further understanding of the customer directly is through knowing the environment and a connection with employees. Employees that are directly involved with selling to customers have an understanding of what they want. Even though it is an indirect approach, connecting with employees and a sales floor presence will bring you closer to the customer.

The third and most important way to understand a customer base is by simply talking to customers. Store Managers typically have time allotted in the day to walk the sales floor. It is inexcusable for a manager at any level to walk by customers without recognition. Some of the best Store Managers have large personalities on the sales floor. They smile and say hello to customers. You would be surprised at how many customers you would get to know by simply acknowledging them. This does not mean taking over the role of sales person, rather, being directional and thanking them for their business.

Store Managers that want to get to know customers must be among them. You cannot hide out in an office all day and believe you have a finger on the pulse of the business. To make the customer a truly significant part of the vision, you must lead by example. There are many instances where employees or managers walk by customers and do not acknowledge them. Store Managers included. It should not be a surprise if you do not recognize customers that your people will not either. They are simply following the lead. You should thank customers often and be a visible presence on the sales floor.

Employees/ Environment

In Chapter 2, we discussed connecting with people and understanding established norms. These two ideas fit perfectly as identifiers. You have to connect with employees. This goes beyond sales numbers on a page. You have to make them a part of the team. This does not mean crossing ethical or policy lines, rather, relating to the team.

Employees have to be coached, trained and developed to succeed and offer the best service. A Store Manager cannot do this nor should they on their own. This development should reach two levels, one level for management staff and another for employees. Connecting with people is not hard to do. You should be present on the sales floor at some point during the day. As you are making your rounds, you should have short and simple conversations with members of the staff.

The conversations should not be solely business focused. They should be a mix of personal and business conversations. The focus should be on what is important to the employee. It may include ways to improve business to what they did on vacation. It is necessary to connect without the employee or managers feeling fear. You cannot use this time to discipline or create goals. The point is to relate to the team. The conversations do not need to take a long time. You have many things on your plate. The connections need to be consistent. You cannot relate to your team this month and next month use the time to berate them.

This method does not negate disciplinary measures. Discipline should be handled separately and in private. This also is not designed for you to become soft or a doormat for people. You have to maintain a down the middle approach. You have to be able to balance the other identifiers and connect with people.

Connecting with people will enable three things in your store:

1. **A hard working, unified and developed team that will work towards the vision.**
2. **Keeps you in sync with the environment and norms.**
3. **Keeps you informed of customer experiences and trends.**

When you connect with people in a way that blends business and fragments of their personal life, it creates a higher sense of loyalty and commitment from the team. If you have worked for an awful boss in the past, chances are they did not balance connecting with people properly. They may have been focused on numbers and not how to achieve a desired performance through valuing people. They could also be too soft and let employees get away with everything, which will kill morale and dampen results. There has to be a balance.

Connecting with your team and coaching your managers to connect with their employees will assist with developing the team. This creates a more desirable work environment and reduces turnover. It also allows you to gain insight into developmental needs of your team. It brings you closer to the team. It brings you into the fold in developing norms and weeding out unproductive behaviors.

Connecting with people helps to bring you closer to understanding the customer base. The closest people to the customers are typically the sales teams and Department Managers. They can provide valuable information about what the customer likes and how they make buying decisions. They are more in-sync with barriers that influence sales negatively. They act as a conduit from the customer to decision makers. Do not undervalue their perspective or potential contribution to servicing customers.

Presentation/ Assortment

Another key identifier to business success or potential failure is the presentation and assortment available in the store. This may seem like an obvious choice. Of course, stores need to have a clean and neat environment for customers to feel welcomed and want to buy. This goes beyond general cleanliness of the store and employees. A clean environment should be a given in any location. The actual presentation may be totally, in part or completely out of a Store Managers control.

In most major retail chains, there are guidelines for the presentation of products. For example, there are dedicated end caps and bulk stacks that must be executed. There may be vendors paying for the space or the company may make significant purchases that must be represented. Some efforts are also in support of advertised items or price/ product impression. You may have autonomy within your store or may have to follow strict disciplines.

The presentation of products should be included in decision-making to determine success or failure rates. This should be done at three levels:

1. **Are presentation standards executed to company standards?**
2. **If you have flexibility, are the "right" items featured?**
3. **Is daily maintenance and in-stock conditions a factor?**

These questions are designed to get into the mind of the customer and see the presentation, as they would experience it. If you have flexibility with presentation, how is the team making decisions? For example, a manager is reviewing reports and notices that kitchen tabletop appliances such as coffeemakers and blenders are trending below sales from the previous year. The first identifier to look at is the presentation of this area. You should walk to this area as a first step observation. Some of the questions I would look to answer are:

- **How is the overall presentation? (Neat, clean, organized, displays, priced, accessible).**
- **Is the presentation set to company guidelines or plans?**
- **Are the shelves full, are the areas being replenished according to company guidelines?**

- **Are there any noticeable barriers or obstructions that may lead to a decline?**

The questions are a starting point. You may have the flexibility with ordering different quantities or models and that may correct the issue. If quantities and models are locked in to the current presentation, you need to consider other identifiers. This step is about seeing the merchandise as the customer does. The presentation may be in the wrong location or informational signage may be lacking. If you cannot control those issues, focus on what you can control. How can you or the staff identify the noticeable issues and determine other identifiers to further investigate or to further success?

This also applies to areas that may be doing well. You may notice an upsurge in a line, but it may be despite what the store is doing. There may be problematic aspects to the presentation, which is hindering further success in the line.

Inventory assortment is another area to consider in conjunction with the presentation. This is another area where you may have limited control. This must be a consideration from the viewpoint of a customer. If the store is out of stock or there is insufficient stock, it may impact the line. If a home improvement store is not local market focused, it may not sell items that are required to meet a state building code and will lose sales. If you have the ability to review your inventory and tailor it to your market, it is another great place to promote growth.

Of course, smart decisions have to be made. For example, an item a manager requests to stock may carry a price tag at twice the price of competitors. The business segment may not provide the right growth. It may be a profit drain sitting on the shelf.

Competition

When investigating reasons for a decline or increase, the competition is often overlooked. We tend to focus solely on internal influences such as inventory or employee training to justify an issue. We ignore external influences that impact the business. This stems from an ego that exists in the competitive world of managers. There is a tendency to believe that a manager's store is the best and there are not competitors that can satisfy a customer better. Though it is great to want to be the best, you must be realistic.

This has been stated before, but it is worth repeating. It is inexcusable for you to ignore the influence and power of competitors. Store Managers have to know what the competition offers. This goes beyond merchandise to the environment and service that customers encounter. You have to understand the environment and programs of competitive retailers to gain insight into why a customer would choose the store.

If we use the same example of a deficit in tabletop appliances, consider the competition in this scenario. Here are some things to review when considering a competitor from a customer's perspective.

- **What does the presentation look like (Neat, clean, organized, priced, in stock)?**
- **How does their pricing compare with your store?**
- **How educated are the employees with selling the items?**
- **How does their assortment differ from your store (more high end/ low end)?**
- **What products are they featuring on end caps/ promotional displays?**
- **What have their advertising/ marketing efforts included (Have they been aggressively advertising this area)?**

These considerations can have an influence on your store. You may find everything internally is running well, but there is still a difference in sales. The competition may be the key for at least some of the difference for better or worse. If they have become aggressive or have let things go, it may show in your sales.

Processes

This is an area that may make things easier or tougher for a customer. Processes can range from everything such as receiving merchandise, stocking the shelves, employee training, point of sale procedures, warranty sales and loading assistance to name a few. These variables can make a difference in where customers decide to buy. The processes in your store are probably regulated by company policy, but how you execute them may determine future visits from a customer.

Your connection with employees will determine the sense of urgency in handling processes. If you never speak to the employee that loads cars, what does the employee think about the value of the position? How eager is the loader going to be to make an impression on the customer? The loader or cashier is typically the last interaction that customers have with a store. If you treat them as expendable, they will live up to the expectations. This may seem more like connecting with people versus processes, but processes are executed by people.

There are two things to consider. The first is if the processes are being completed according to company guidelines. The second is how you motivate the team to complete the process. The entire management team is responsible for recognizing gaps in process execution. If the receiving process is broken it will affect the ability to fill the shelves, which may equate to lost sales. If cashiers are not offering warranties with eligible items, it may decrease customer satisfaction with the product.

Processes improvement is overlooked because managers feel processes are set in stone by corporate leaders. Store Managers assume processes cannot be influenced. This is incorrect. Your actual ability to create or change policy may be non-existent. The ability to influence people is within your control. Your ability to execute and provide a better customer experience than your competitor is within your control. You may identify an opportunity area and discover the presentation is right, your store is competitive, environment is solid, customers like the product and your offering, but your replenishment process may be missing sales by identifying an empty shelf too late.

Consultative View

Everything comes back to the two main questions asked at the beginning of this chapter.

1. **How is the problem influencing the components of the business?**
2. **How are the components of the business creating the problem?**

You need to step back from the problem to evaluate the underlying causes. The identifiers are a quick analysis to begin the process. If you leave out an identifier, you may be leaving the cause of an issue in place. Managerial analysis must be more thorough than a rushed decision. You cannot look at a successful line and hope to find out why it is performing well without running through the various elements that influence it.

The identifiers should be a part of your daily through pattern. When you recognize an issue that you want to work on, you should immediately run through the primary identifiers. When you are dealing with more complex problems, there will be a more in depth process.

A consultant will dive much deeper than what is presented in this chapter. The business identifiers are a less formal way to determine needs. This should go beyond Store Managers to the entire managerial staff. If an Assistant Manager identifies a problem, they should have a way to analyze it to create solutions. If your staff is making decisions based on limited analysis, the problem will continue to haunt the store. If there are areas that are performing well, they should know why to enable the store to capitalize on the success.

CHAPTER 4

THE RETAIL CONSULTING PRINCIPLES

There is a method or flow to analyzing a problem and creating solutions. You cannot shorten the process or skip around it and expect a long-term solution to last. This differs from a consultant's path by eliminating the negotiating and contracting phases of consulting. These phases have consultants navigating the expectations and entering into a contract with a business.

There are six components that comprise the retail consulting principles. They represent a further analysis of consulting and progressive steps that are adapted to the retail environment. The components represent the solution process from recognition of a problem to creating lasting change.

- **State the Problem**
- **Managerial Diagnosis**

- **Discovery & Fact Finding**
- **Connecting the Whole System**
- **Solutions**
- **Buy-In & Long-Term Change**

The list may seem overwhelming, but you can flow through the process at a fluid pace to produce a view of the entire state of the problem. The steps are expanded to allow for managers at varied levels, and experience to follow the process. Some experienced managers may move through the first four steps at a smoother pace than inexperienced or new managers. Regardless, the fact building process leads to developing solutions, which requires time to create.

The properties of each step lead you to the next part of the process. It is a case building perspective. It gathers the facts and fills in the missing pieces of the puzzle to stimulate thought around solutions. You need to have all of the pieces in place to develop a solution with long-term implications. The puzzle will not be complete until the solution piece and buy-in piece are positioned. It will take time after a solution is implemented to determine the real value of the process.

Step 1: State the Problem

Stating the problem goes beyond simply saying here is the issue. In a lot of cases you will not understand the true nature of the problem. Store Managers may know that sales have declined in the bedding department with no real structurally based reason as to why it is happening. They are taking their gut instinct at this point and using it as a working understanding of the problem.

You are developing your own sense of the problem. This is familiar territory for managers. They apply their initial thought or gut instinct to problems every day. You may be tempted to create a hypothesis to apply to the situation, be cautious of this action. A hypothesis is a specific statement that users try to prove or disprove through fact-finding and diagnosis. You are viewing the problem through a narrow lens to determine if your feelings of the problem are accurate. For example, a manager may believe that sales in bedding have declined because of price increases that recently took place. They work on this premise to determine the accuracy of the hypothesis.

The problem with hypothesizing in retail is it will narrow your view and you may miss something during your discovery step to creating solutions. For example, a manager is focusing on the price increase in bedding as the culprit to the declining sales. They may miss facts such as confusing signage for customers, inadequate training for employees, inventory levels or out of stock functions. They are pursuing one aspect of the problem and changing the hypothesis as new information is discovered.

The statement of the problem should be general in nature. You are working towards a full understanding of the problem. You should grab a notebook to begin your quest for answers. You should enter each step as you go along. The top of the page is where your statement should preside. For example, *"The sales in the bedding department have declined 6% this year."* You do not need to value add or extend the thought. You will be diagnosing the issue and uncovering facts along the way. If you have specific areas that you want to ensure are included, you should jot them down, as well. For example, you may make a note that highlights pricing and inventory to ensure these areas are explored.

The statement is recognition that a problem exists. It is a brief summation of the issue or concern. It is the working title of the consulting project. The rest of the steps in the consulting process will provide further information about contributors to the problem. The final steps will provide an answer to the question found in the statement.

Step 2: Managerial Diagnosis

This step will have you asking questions about the statement. You are preparing the statement for discovery and fact-finding. This step is more of a self-diagnosis. You are challenging the original statement. The four interrelated components that comprise this step are:

- What proof is there that the problem exists?
- Why does the problem exists?
- What impact has the problem had on the whole system?
- What are the known specifics related to the problem?

The questions are designed to get you thinking a little deeper about the situation. It moves you from thinking about the generalities of the problem to analyzing the foundation and effects of the problem. These questions do not require a major investment of time, but they do require seeking answers beyond the tip of the iceberg that is seen. Store Managers need to begin looking beneath the surface.

What proof is there that the problem exists? This should be an easy question. It is asking how you came to the determination that there is a problem. Most discoveries are made through reporting. You may notice a downward slide in a department or product group. This should be an observation of an occurring trend. If a department or product group has a couple of bad weeks, it may not be anything but a bump in the road. If you are making a comparison to a performance from last year take into consideration seasonal trends, calendar shifts and promotional efforts. There may have been a promotion last year, which accounted for the uptick in sales performance. There will more than likely be several issues that need to be addressed. Prioritize the issues and focus your efforts where there is the most to gain.

Why does this problem exist? This question is asking how the problem came to be. You may not have a definitive answer. You do not have all of the facts yet. This question is closely related to the statement. The obvious leap here is any recent change that may have influenced or created the problem. There are times that you will find that a change and decline are coincidental. A change in the pricing structure of the bedding department may not be the driving force behind the 6% decline in sales. You should ask why this change is happening. What are the surface explanations?

What impact has the problem had on the whole system? This question will get you thinking beyond your initial impression of the problem. The assessment of a problem is probably based on a numerical performance. You can see the immediate result of a problem such as declining sales in a product group. You need to expand your view to influences on both internal and external sources. How has this problem affected other elements such as adjacent product groups or add-on sales? How have internal and external sources contributed to the problem? You need to consider the problem from both perspectives. A great method to examine the problem is to connect it to the other elements. Draw a box on a piece of paper with the problem statement and connect it to other boxes that represent areas that are touched by the problem. This will give you a visual representation and distance from the problem emotionally.

What are the known specifics related to the problem? This part of the diagnosis process gathers all of the data known about the problem and the whole system. These are facts, not assumptions that are at the surface. You are not digging beneath the surface at this point. All of the information that led you to pursue a solution to the problem should be organized. Consider the information that influences the problem, this aligns with proof that the problem exists. The difference is adding the proof that surrounds or contributes to the problem, as well. This should also include the policies and procedures that are violated or not in use. If you are not following a policy, it may be influencing your results negatively.

Step 3: Discovery & Fact Finding

This is an observation step in the process. This is an opportunity to take what you have learned from your initial assumption and surface data and dig deeper. This step is where you unravel the mystery that surrounds the problem. There are several elements that comprise the discovery and fact-finding step.

- **Gather data**
- **Analyze the depth of the problem**
- **Determine contributors to the problem**

- **Determine the gaps between the desired state and actual state**
- **Decide what must change**

There is a lot to do during this step in the process. There will also be a considerable amount of time wrapped up during the fact-finding phase. This step is the rest of the iceberg that hides beneath the surface of the water. It is essential to get this part right. If you cut corners or rush through it, you will not see the rest of the iceberg beneath the water, and the problem will remain. You need to know why the problem exists to apply a long-term remedy.

Gather data. Store Managers need to be organized and methodical when approaching the subject of gathering statistics and data. You need to start with the surface data that was gathered in acknowledgement of the problem. This is usually a high-level view of the problem such as a department that has declined in sales. Now, take the department and break it down in to factors such as product lines. This will depend widely on what reporting is available. The greater depth in reporting, the deeper you can dig. You should consider staffing reports, on-hand/ in-stock reports, trending reports and others that touch the department or problem. You need to look beyond printed reports to other elements, as well. What have you observed in the department? Is the department stocked efficiently? Is the staff scheduled at peak times and are they trained? Are the presentation standards aligned with company expectations? What did you observe with customer service? Consider the customer feedback given to the staff on product assortment and pricing. What have you learned about competitive influences in this area? Take the problem and pick it apart, be as finite as possible. You should keep your supporting materials organized and take notes of observations. Ensure you also gather information on all policies and procedures that relate to your problem. You need to construct solutions within the parameters established by the organization.

Analyze the depth of the problem. Once you have all of the supporting documentation, you can move forward. Analyze the depth of the problem with a goal of peeling back the layers to determine the broad impact. You should try to piece together a mini-history of when the problem began, if possible, and when. This part should not take much time. You are piecing together the information to create a timeline and notice changes in the landscape. This may help you determine contributors to the problem or other influences that have created a negative change. You should approach this part with the idea of learning more about how the problem has impacted the store.

Determine contributors to the problem. This part looks for who and what has influenced the problem. This is where your depth analysis from the last part will be utilized to isolate contributors to the problem. Who or what contributed to this decline or problem?

Who is used as a broad term, it could be your own company or competition. It could be your stocking crew or sales team. The who or what could be a combination of many things that led to the current result. Assistant Managers need to create a list to help in the solution phase of consulting. Store Managers cannot gain an understanding of the problem if they do not know the contributing forces to it. If you skip this part, you will be creating solutions that fall into the same cycle. The same contributors will be present. The contributors can also be broader such as the market, trends, inventory levels, pricing, web competition, location in the store, etc. Do not move forward with a generic list. Create the list of all possible elements and move forward with contributors that seem applicable to the problem.

Determine the gaps between the desired state and actual state. You have gathered data and analyzed it as well as determined contributors. You have developed a picture of where the store is (actual state) and in some cases how the store got there. Now, you need to determine what the desired state looks like. If the problem were fixed or never existed, what would be seen? Think of this in realistic terms and within the resources that are available. You cannot create a dream state with a huge staff and advanced technology if that is not within the parameters of possibility.

The goal of this exercise is to determine what needs to be integrated into solutions. This will close the gap between the desired and actual state. The gap is what you need to do to get to the desired state. This examination also looks at the things that the store is doing well. Because there is a problem area, does not mean that every element that comprises the situation is broken. The list from this exercise must state what needs to be accomplished to obtain the desired state. The list should be broken out by what the store is doing well and opportunities.

Decide what must change. You have put the research to good use. You applied deep thought to determine the gaps that exist between the desired and actual state. Now, you need to determine what must change to get to the desired state. We discussed that your team will be doing things well, and these efforts should not be discarded. There needs to be a focus on what needs to change to get to the desired state. The next step will be connecting your change to the whole system, so it is critical that you leave this step with a detailed list of the changes required. This list must be based on current resources and within the guidelines of company policy. This is another area that must be based on reality. You cannot decide that the computer system must change. It will not happen. You need to think within the authorized guidelines. You are not trying to create a new department or a new version of something. You need to follow the company initiative and follow procedures. If a you stray from company guidelines, the change will not stick and you may violate policies and endure the penalty that goes along with it.

Step 4: Connecting the Whole System

This step takes your determination of what must change and connects it to the whole system. We discussed the whole system earlier to include the internal and external environment. The whole system is comprised of customers, employees, resources, expenses, policies, areas that surround the problem or interest, competition, as well as merchandising and brands. Take your decisions of what must change and connect them to the whole system. If you decide staffing was a contributor to the problem, and the gap exists, connect it to the environment. If there is a need to shift hours and take them away from another department how does this change affect the store? How does it affect customer service both positively and negatively? How will it influence the employees? What are the other gaps that would be filled by additional staffing? How will decisions gain a competitive edge? How will expenses be impacted and handled? Take out your paper and pencil and draw a box that states your need for change. Connect the box to all of the other elements that exist within the whole system touched by the decision. This offers a visual representation of potential barriers and influences of the decision or on the decision.

Step 5: Solutions

All of the work and discovery will help during this crucial step. The whole point of going through all of the steps is to create solutions. Keep in mind that solutions must be within company policies and guidelines. Even internal or external consultants must work within boundaries. Store Managers cannot create "cowboy" programs that stray from the needs and demands of the organization and expect good results. The policies and procedures should have been gathered during the data and fact-finding step.

Creating solutions are a culmination of work and reflection. Reflection is a practice of looking back at past decisions to influence future results. It requires dedicated time to think about the problem and any experiences from your past connected with it. You may think about a direct or indirect experience such as learning through a past supervisor. If nothing is related to the problem, you will need to rely on research. Here are a few suggestions.

- **Reflect on the problem and past experiences.**
- **List all known elements that exist including policy and procedures.**
- **Run your ideas through the whole system check.**
- **Create an alternate solution for validation.**
- **Create a detailed solution plan that includes implementation steps and key players.**

When beginning the process, you should list all of the known elements. You should have an understanding, through all of your work, the policies and procedures that must be followed, staffing requirements, basics or standard processes and what is working and broken. You must stop and ask if you can create solutions based on the minimums required by the company. For example, if your problem is an employee turnover problem in the lighting department, can it be repaired for the long-term by simply following all of the policies or is there additional work that must be done. Maybe there is a need for additional training or goals assigned to the team. There may be opportunities in training for the manager of that area to enhance their skills. If you can repair the issue for the long-term, what is the plan to ensure the store does not stray from the basics again to allow the problem to reappear?

When you have given thought to some ideas that may work, there is a need to run them through the whole system check. Draw a box on paper and connect your thoughts to all elements it may touch. It is ok to have barriers that arise; you need to determine if employees can overcome them. Store Managers should not be thinking about how to get around a barrier. Working around barriers does not solve the problem; it postpones and creates other problems. The idea may come up against a policy and will not be able to work. You should anticipate barriers and roadblocks; they come with the territory of planning change.

The retail consulting principles will mainly be used on large or complex problems. It is unlikely that you will go through all of the steps for simple, immediate issues. This aligns with the notion that your company would only hire a consultant for multi-faceted problems. The issues may be problems connected to other problems that require multiple solutions. You may encounter other, less visible, problems while connecting the whole system. You need to continually work ideas through the whole system check to find ones with barriers that can be removed and achieve the desired state.

You have to create a workable strategy through identifying its ability to achieve the desired state. You need to go back to the drawing board one more time. Creating an alternate solution is not busy work or a fall back plan. It is taking another idea, running it through the whole system check to accomplish one of two things. It will either validate the original plan as the most effective or may suggest the alternate plan may be more satisfactory. This will happen in a lot of cases. You get the creative juices flowing and can enhance the original idea by adding or subtracting an element you did not think of before.

After a manager has analyzed the solution, there is a need to create a detailed solution plan. Create a detailed solution plan by stating the step-by-step implementation of the plan including key players. What is going to be done and who is accountable for each step. The plan should outline the problem, the specifics of the problem and the goals. Here are some of the inclusions for a detailed written plan:

- **Problem statement.**
- **Actual state and desired state.**
- **Explain each step in detail.**
- **Specify time lines and roles.**
- **Schedule milestone checkpoints to review progress.**
- **Gauge success.**

A Store Manager also needs to schedule milestone checkpoints. These are scheduled meetings to review progress and determine if adjustments are required. This strengthens employee buy-in, but it also ensures the plan is implemented and not forgotten. You should keep the written plan as a guide throughout the process. You should also have the whole system connection worksheet available at all times. During the checkpoints, you will be able to add and takeaway for barriers that were overcome and unforeseen problems that arise.

This step is comparable to plans that internal and external consultants offer their clients. The consultant offers the manager a detailed plan for two reasons. First, the plan serves as a roadmap for the manager to use to strengthen their environment and fix the problem. Second, the plan serves as a current lesson, and one to utilize in the future. The consultant is helping the managers help themselves in the future. The plan for an external consultant is more of a collaborative effort rather than a one-way conversation. The consultant offers the path and the manager adjusts it for their environment.

The plan must include the elements you will use to gauge success. The state you are working towards is the desired state, but how will you know you are progressing or when you get there? You need to specify the reports you will use, the observations required and solicited feedback along with sources that will supply the feedback. You may not think it is necessary to spell this out. Plans that do not include a measure for success may determine success has occurred too early or never realize it happened.

The Store Manager is the retail consultant for their building. It is your responsibility to analyze problems and create solutions for lasting change. You have a store full of employees. The company is dependent upon you to overcome obstacles. Think about a managerial position, a great portion of the job is resolving conflict and solving problems. If you solve critical problems with intelligent, well-informed solutions, it will strengthen your environment. The morale in your store will improve along with the commitment of your team.

Step 6: Buy-In & Long-Term Change

Your consultative pursuit should align with the vision of the organization. Your company has established a clearly defined message. The vision or mission statement should be readily available to everyone in the organization including shareholders. Everything accomplished in a store should move the organization towards the visionary goal. The vision statement is typically vague and includes providing outstanding customer service. You should gain employee commitment in conjunction with the vision statement to create a consistent message.

The vision of the organization is one element to help link the efforts of change with the efforts of your people. You need to understand if your plans are successful or have failed. This can only be accomplished through diverse points of view. During the implementation and after the implementation it is good to include a diverse mix of people. This really has nothing to do with ethnicity. This is referring to a diverse mix of experiences. For example, members of your team with various specialties such as selling, administrative or facilities are gathered together to discuss the implementation. As stated, the true measure of success of an initiative is when opposing views agree the problem is resolved for the long-term. Your collection of team members will be comprised of some that see the value in the initiative while others will not agree with the plan. When these differing views can agree the change and implementation are successful, there is a better chance it will last.

A factor to anticipate during any change initiative is resistance. When you make a radical change or even get back to the basics, you will encounter push back. Your plans will interrupt established norms and a comfort level with employees. There will be a portion of the population that challenges the new plan through resistance. The best way to reduce resistance is by including members of the team in the implementation process and constant communication. If you include key members of the team that represent the store population in decision-making, it will produce a higher level of commitment. Before the implementation begins, assemble a small team and discuss the initiative. Listen to the team's ideas and suggestions, they understand the norms, and they are closer to the customer. Communication to the entire team is vital throughout change. They need to understand how the change aligns with their work and vision. Honest, open communication is a necessity during change.

Even after the initiative has been implemented, it requires ongoing care and review. You need the buy-in from the team to solve a problem and fix something for the long-term. Provide the team with progress updates and adjustments that become necessary. Communicate the good and bad of the initiative and foster open lines of two-way communication to continually validate success.

Remember, the desired state is the goal. Store Managers must continually monitor the progress of the plan until successful integration has occurred. After success has been determined, you should validate the plan periodically. This does not typically happen in retail. Once problems appear to be resolved, you move on to put out the next fire. There is a good chance you will monitor developing problems in situations where you have created solutions. This is an ongoing process. The process will pay continual dividends because the change is for the long-term and the whole system.

CHAPTER 5

TRAINING WHEELS

This chapter will present a case study of a retail store with potential problems. Some of the problems will be at the surface while others will be harder to see. You will put on the hat of a retail consultant to diagnose problems and offer solutions. Your role will be an external consultant. There are details included about the environment and others will be assumed.

There are no absolute answers. Store Managers view, react and resolve issues differently. What may work for one manager may not work for another. What is required to arrive at a solution is an analysis of the retail consulting principles.

- **State the Problem**
- **Managerial Diagnosis**
- **Discovery & Fact Finding**

- Connecting the Whole System
- Solutions
- Buy-In & Long-Term Change

When Store Managers integrate the retail consulting principles into their ability to assess a situation, the analysis is thorough. Review the situation, take notes and begin the process. It will be easier to remove emotions from the case study because there is no personal investment. You should begin to realize that reviewing your store as a business will yield similar results.

This case study is an opportunity to test the consulting training wheels. The wheels will soon come off, and you will continue to develop your skills. The study will provide enough information to lay a foundation for generating solutions.

Case Study

Background: Mary Stevenson (pseudo name) is the Store Manager of unit #1722 for the retail chain Dollars and Bargains (pseudo name). The retailer first opened its doors in the late 1980's. It has grown through recent rapid expansion to over 2,000 locations. They are smaller stores, approx 15,000 square feet with a general assortment of goods. They position themselves as a value priced retailer for price conscious shoppers. The recent recession has brought a lot of business and attention to the stores as customers seek alternatives to save money and stretch their budget. They cater to the female shopper, which represents 61% of their total business.

The unit opened in 2008, and Mary became the Store Manager in 2011. Prior to this assignment, she was an Assistant Manager in a smaller store. She has been with the company since 2007 and started as the Assistant Manager in a smaller unit. She has been in various managerial roles, in an 11 year career. She had worked for big box retailers in various capacities. This is her first assignment as a Store Manager.

The store has been steadily declining over the past year. The store ended last year off by (6%) and declined this year after the first quarter. The store currently has declined another (2.3%) in comparable sales. The store is missing its sales goal in comparison to last year and is missing the established budget by (4.6%). Here is how key department performance finished for the year:

- **Books (.3%)**
- **House wares 1.9%**
- **Domestics (3.8%)**
- **Carpet (2.6%)**
- **Food/ Pantry 1.2%**
- **Hardware (1.4%)**

- **Personal Care 4.1%**
- **Clothing 2.2%**
- **Toys (1.0%)**
- **Automotive (3.1%)**
- **Furniture .5%**

The margin has remained comparable to last year at 32%. Expenses in the store have increased by 3%. The surrounding stores experienced moderate increases during the last year. The store stands out as a struggling unit in her district. Mary has reviewed the numbers, and she understands the departments that have contributed to the problem. She had conversations with the Department Managers of domestics and automotive which she considers that major contributors to the sales decline. The conversations have not resulted in any improvement, and Mary is seeking guidance to understand the sales decline and develop solutions.

You are part of the external consulting team in this exercise. You are asked to evaluate the process, and create solutions. You will come along with the store visit and conversations with key staff members. You should utilize the retail consulting principles and think through the decisions. The consulting session is set for two days. The first will be interviews and data gathering. The second day is dedicated to observation and analysis.

Day One: The first day began with an interview with Mary, the Store Manager. We asked several questions to determine her thoughts on the problem. Mary did not offer much insight into the contributors to the issue. She was looking at the problems from the surface. She states, *"The store continues to decline. I see the departments that contribute to the decline. They are evident through sales reporting."* Mary had discussions with the Department Managers of domestics and automotive. Mary said, *"I told the Department Managers to dig into the product lines that were declining. They were to review the lines and ensure the visual presentation and signage was up to standard."* Mary validated that the process was complete and further directed the managers to focus on the declining product lines.

We had an understanding of the problem and what the Store Manager did to overcome the issue. We determined that the two departments showing the largest decline was the best place to start. We included carpet as an opportunity, as well. We proceeded to set up times to interview an assortment of individuals. The list we came up with is the following:

- **Amy, the Department Manager of Domestics**
- **Dale, the Department Manager of Automotive**
- **Jessica, the Customer Service Manager**
- **Robert, the Receiving Manager**

- **Sue, Sales Associate in Domestics**
- **Jim, Sales Associate in Automotive**
- **Larry, Stocking Associate for multiple areas in the store**
- **Scott, the Department Manager of Carpet**

We felt these individuals would offer a fair representation of the store as a whole. The entire staff consists of 40 individuals with eight being the focus of the interviews.

Sue: We started with the Sales Associates. This allowed us to get an accurate picture of life on the sales floor. Sue was very open with her frustration on the sales front. She said, *"We are never staffed right. I know customers get frustrated because they have to wait and some leave."* She was unsure if the perceived staffing issue is a lack of people or erroneous scheduling. When we asked Sue about merchandise she stated, *"We seem ok on inventory, there are times we run out of stock on advertised items, but for the most part it is ok."* We thanked Sue and moved on to the next interview.

Jim: Jim has been with the store since it had opened with all of his experience in automotive supplies. He began with the working relationship between Dale, the supervisor, and him. They have worked together for years. Jim stated, *"Dale works hard on being in-stock, we are rarely light on inventory unless it is just not available."* When asked about staffing and coverage, he said, *"We* seem to be able to handle the business, I believe we are fully staffed." We continued to question Jim, looking for any signs of issues that may contribute to the problem, we asked about competitors. The team had not been inside of the competition in quite some time, but they felt good about their service and customer base.

Dale: We moved on to Dale, the Automotive Manager. He believed the staffing matrix and the scheduling was according to company guidelines. We asked Dale about his department and his perception of the problems that have led to the decrease in his area. Dale stated, *"We are pretty much left alone in automotive. We do not see Mary at all."* He continued, *"We know the business pretty well, we have a loyal customer base, our customer count has declined but we feel the customers will be back."* Dale also validated the in-stock condition and showed his process for monitoring it closely.

Amy: Amy, the Department Manager of Domestics was scheduled next. She validated that there were no staffing shortage in the department over the past year. She stated, *"We had no problems over the past year keeping the department staffed. We move around hours sometimes when there is a shortage in other parts of the store."* We discussed one of the concerns that Sue had with inventory shortages on advertised items. Amy was not aware of any problems with inventory. We also asked about her support system. Amy stated, *"We see Mary occasionally. She offers support, and we had a conversation about the sales issues."*

Robert: Robert is the Receiving Manager and we wanted to get his perspective on merchandise receiving in the target departments and product flow to the sales floor. Robert stated, *"The method to receive goods in automotive or hard goods is much easier than soft goods. Domestics are time consuming due to all of the style variations and alternate skus. It is a much more challenging process. It creates delays getting merchandise to the floor."* He admits the process in domestics could be improved, but they do not have the time to dedicate to improving the function. Another point taken from the conversation is the frequency for soft goods. There is one additional truck every week for soft goods than the other departments.

Jessica: Jessica is the Customer Service Manager and the goal was learning about service levels in general and in the target departments. Jessica stated, *"We have received complaints from customers on the service times in domestics. Automotive and carpet get complaints rarely, and it has to do with price matching competitors and pricing."* Jessica could not recall any compliments in regards to service in the target areas. She also stated, *"We have been trying to improve service throughout the store. We are discussing customer service more because of the sales decrease. We are also educating the sales teams on our price* *matching policy."*

Larry: Larry is a stocking/replenishment associate that works early shifts. We wanted to get a feeling for the mentality of the stocking team. We asked Larry about replenishing the domestic department. He stated, *"The team does not like replenishing domestics. There are multiple sku's for an individual item such as draperies or table covers. It is time consuming; we try to leave that department to last. Whatever we do not get done during our shift goes to the sales floor team."* We asked about automotive and other areas such as carpeting, and there were no concerns on behalf of the team.

Scott: Scott is the Carpet Department Manager and we decided to review this business because it represents a 2.6% sales decline. When we asked why there was a decrease in carpeting, Scott stated, *"There was a new competitor that opened last year that took some of the business. We had some staffing issues last year, but they are rectified. My biggest concern is our pricing. We are not competitive right now. The competition kills us on pricing."* There were no inventory issues or replenishing issues in the department.

We completed the interviews that were scheduled and organized the notes. We asked the Store Manager to retrieve reporting that may help us gain further insight into the issues. She printed the reports, and we got to work sorting through the material. We asked for brief explanations and began building the puzzle piece by piece.

Data Gathering: We began by looking at sales volumes by department. We could see the obvious contributors to the decline. The domestics department was down (3.8%) with $500k in sales. The automotive department was down (3.1%) with $275k in sales. We looked at carpet as well, with a (2.6%) loss in comparison to the previous year and $3.2MM in sales. The entire store generated $12MM last year.

We took note of the product categories that were contributing to the decline year end, last year.:

- **Bedding (7.0%)**
- **Draperies (4.1%)**
- **Automotive Specialty (2.3%)**
- **Stock Carpet (3.8%)**
- **Kitchen Flooring (2.1%)**

We reviewed staffing reports for the store. We took note of the target areas:

- **Domestics (Vacant position, 1 part time sales)**

- **Automotive (Vacant positions, 1 full time sales)**
- **Carpet (Vacant positions, 2 part time sales, 1 part time loader)**
- **Receiving (Vacant positions, 0 full or part time)**
- **Stocking/ Replenishment (Vacant positions 1 full time, 1 part time)**

The company has a Department Manager Walk Notes Program. The Assistant Managers are supposed to walk the department with the Department Manager, and provide presentation standards and inventory tasks for the team. The sheets should be completed every two weeks. They should be filed for review by the Store Manager. The following are the completion timeframes of the last reports.

- **Domestics (Last completion was two months ago).**
- **Automotive (Current through last week).**
- **Carpet (Last completion was four months ago).**
- **Receiving (N/A).**
- **Stocking/ Replenishment (No copies of the paperwork were filed).**

We reviewed the company guidelines on replenishing the sales floor. The merchandise flow matrix lists soft lines areas replenished before other areas of the stores. The areas are more complex but depend on availability and presence of new colors and patterns. These areas are merchandised and displayed to the female shopper, which represent 61% of the stores total business. The carpet department has a priority for hard lines. It represents the largest volume in most stores.

The store had no succession plan, and the overall turnover ratio was 1.5% higher than last year. Customer complaints are rated by calls or emails through a specific number and email address. The store was higher in customer complaints by 2.0% over last year. The reports did not breakdown the element by department or area.

There were no additional reports available. We completed the research through the available reports. We organized the findings and prepared for the observations that would take place on day two. The goal was gathering as much factual information as possible that would support proposed solutions.

Day Two: We begin the second day prepared for visual observations of several key areas. We will start early and review the replenishment process, receiving process, domestic sales floor, automotive sales floor and we added the carpet sales area, as well. We will spend a small amount of time in each area, ask questions along the way and summarize thoughts.

Replenishment: We reviewed the process of taking the loaded carts from the receiving area to the sales floor. The team is comprised of 4 associates, 3 men and 1 woman. The men gravitated to the hard line goods. They worked independently in these areas. This included the automotive area. The female replenishment team member started with clothing and moved into house wares. The domestic's area was last and did not get completed. They are not directly supervised. The opening manager lets them inside of the building. The team makes the decisions on what areas to complete first.

Receiving: There was one small truck being unloaded in receiving. The Department Manager organized the team. They sorted and separated merchandise by department. The goods were staged in a holding area, ready to be taken to the sales floor. The goods stayed in the staging area until the next morning for the replenishment team.

Domestics: The domestics department, the second largest department in the store, in square footage, had two associates on the sales floor for the two hour observation. It was 30 minutes into the observation before a manager took one of the salespeople to cover another area in the store. The department had three customers in the area at the time. The remaining associate continued working on the stock cart placed on the sales floor. The associate stopped her task work when a customer entered the department and asked if they needed help. We witnessed three customers that were not helped while the associate was helping other customers. The associate that was removed did not return during the visit. The presentation looked clean and neat. There were out of stock holes in various areas of the department. The bedding section showed several out of stock locations.

Automotive: The automotive department has general supplies for cars and trucks. It is a smaller department with larger tandems for merchandise. This reduces the sightline for employees to see all of the area. We observed the area for one hour. There was one associate scheduled on the sales floor. There were no stock carts on the floor. The sales person focused on customer service. We did not witness any customers that walked away without help. The customer traffic count was 12 during the hour. The presentation of the department was neat and clean. There were out of stock items, but they were a minimal part of the presentation.

Carpet: The carpet department has three different types of racks. The first are tall racks in the back of the department that contain rolls of stock carpet. The second are eye level, standing racks that hold carpet samples. The third are floor level for area rugs. There was one associate working during the hour long observation. There was one cart on the floor with area rugs to stock. The associate worked on the cart while interacting with customers. The signage in the department was hard to find. It may be missing or the only signage library available. The associate had to refer to his computer system several times during the observation. The department signage may not be set to company standards. The associate was unsure if there were other signs available. There were 4 customers in the department during the hour. The area was clean and neat with a few noticeable out of stock rolls in the stock carpet area.

The observations came to a conclusion, and it was time to wrap all of the information together. We meet as consultants to discuss the findings. There are multiple ways to look at the material and interpret the data. The goal is to be factual and remove emotion. The reason this exercise has you as a consultant is to give you an opportunity to be objective. If you could view your business this way, you may get down to the core problem.

Debrief

Let's get started. The information that was gathered should be plugged into the retail consulting principles that we discussed earlier. The intent of this process is to be a guide for sorting and separating the facts to arrive at a solution. The debrief sessions gathers the materials and your thoughts. Will this be more challenging in your own building? Of course it will. Store Managers are emotionally attached. Think of this store as your new assignment; now look at the facts.

Consider the case study and apply the facts to the consulting principles. You are not looking for solutions at first. It may be difficult because you may feel an understanding of the environment. You may be tempted to apply instant fixes to the problems. Instant fixes will never produce long-term results. How can a manager change the environment? How can a manager change people? What kind of resistance will they encounter? Are you and the Retail Consultants prepared to have an honest discussion with Mary about the store? If you already have the solutions for the store, there continues to be thinking in piece meal terms. You are fixing problems independently, and you may not be connecting the whole system. Take your time to analyze the situation and create a plan to solve the issues in the Bargains and Dollars store. You need to utilize the retail consulting principles.

- **State the Problem**
- **Managerial Diagnosis**
- **Discovery & Fact Finding**
- **Connecting the Whole System**
- **Solutions**
- **Buy-In & Long-Term Change**

Analysis

There are several issues occurring during this example. If this were your store, there would be time and insight into the entire landscape of the building. You may notice other contributing factors that come from opposing corners of the store. This example shows that insight gained through external consulting may not notice established norms or policy infringements or barriers that prevent progression. We will examine each of the six consulting principles.

Step 1: State the Problem

There are concerns that arose during the interviews and observations. These issues were below the surface of what appeared to be the problem. Mary observed the problem from the surface. She also viewed the contributors from the surface, as well. This is what a manager does when stating the problem. Managers do not know any of the details, just the results. The problem in this scenario is a sales decline for the store last year and its continuing effects this year.

The problem statement: *A sales decline in the store last year, which has continued, led by two key departments.* The statement is fundamental but gets to the point of what needs to be resolved. It is a question that needs to be answered. The statement is the starting point that leads to discovery and uncovering truths that exist but naked to the untrained eye. Your statement does not have to mirror this one word for word. The statement should include the sales decline in the store.

Step 2: Managerial Diagnosis

This step is designed to dig deeper into the problems in your store. We will answer the questions of proof and impact through an external lens. The proof of the problem is evident in the numbers reported for the store and the domestics, automotive and carpet departments. There was reporting available for product lines, as well. Another factor to consider is the performance of the store in comparison to others in the district. Mary's store was underperforming when comparing to local units.

This step would be completed before fact-finding. It is meant to help narrow the issue to avoid trying to tackle the entire environment. The initial thoughts on the issue were not only the departments contributed to the loss, but how management contributed to the loss, as well. Mary's only attempt to pin down the variables occurring in the environment was a conversation with two Department Managers. She isolated the entire decrease to two departments, and the message she conveyed to the managers was to fix whatever problems existed.

Mary considered the impact of the department performance as influencing the entire store performance. She never considered other contributing factors. She also identified the domestics department and automotive by percentage and not dollars. She was working on these two departments, which needed guidance, but there was another department that carried significant weight with the problem.

The known specifics of the problem were limited to reporting. Mary did not observe or analyze the environment. Store Managers need to do more in their store. Managers cannot simply recognize a problem and take it at surface value. During this step, think beyond the obvious. Very few problems lie at the surface in their entirety. Most problems only show the result of underlying issues.

Step 3: Discovery & Fact Finding

This is the step where the underlying causes become evident. The information was limited in this case. It is a smaller retailer and may not have all of the resources a big box store possesses. The reports available were store sales, product categories, staffing and the Department Manager Walk Notes Program. The reports were not as effective as the observation and interviews in this case. The data does the job to help with targeting problem areas and significant contributors.

Analysis of the problem led to a determination that managers are not involved in the problem areas. This includes the Store and Department Managers. Throughout three departments analyzed, Mary was not present or involved as a leader. She had limited visibility in the departments that she considered contributors to the decline. The feedback on Mary was offered by the Department Managers. The following are points that confirm the depth of the problem.

Domestics

- ➤ **Staffing:** There is one vacant position in part time sales. There are other issues that exist with staffing the department through observation and interviews. They pull an associate on a regular basis to cover other areas of the store. This creates a shortage in the department. The store turnover ratio is 1.5% higher than last year, though no specific departmental reporting was available.

- ➤ **Customer Service:** The personnel shortage created customer opportunities on the sales floor. We witnessed customers that walked away from the department, and associates validated this level of service as a regular occurrence. Customer complaint numbers for the store had increased 2.0%, though no specific departmental reporting was available. The Customer Service manager reported customer complaints about wait times in the department. The complaints are in line with interviews and observations of the department.

> **Presentation:** The presentation of the department was clean and organized. There were several out of stock items in bedding which ran a (7.0%) last year. The out of stock items diminished the overall presentation of the department. The Department Manager Walk Notes Program that reviews presentation has not been completed in two months. The management staff is inconsistent with the program.

> **Replenishment:** This process is broken, lacks supervision, and is a contributor to the sales decline. The team lacks direction and products are not prioritized. The team dislikes the product and the complexities of sizes and color skus. This creates a delay in getting merchandise to the sales floor which leave empty spaces without product well in to the day.

> **Inventory:** The department has stock condition issues. The team validated a lack of advertised merchandise, which equates to lost sales. The ordering process needs to be explored through management. This will ensure quantities are secured.

> **Receiving:** This process should be reviewed for the domestics department. The unload process is efficient. The merchandise can sit in the staging area for most of a day.

There needs to be a collaborative effort to get merchandise to the sales floor quickly.

Automotive

- **Staffing:** The department is showing a vacancy on the sales floor of one full time sales position. The current staff, including Jim, seems to have a vast array of knowledge of automotive supplies. Dale, the Automotive Manager, was unaware that a vacancy exists. He assumed the area was staffed and following scheduling guidelines. The turnover ratio of the store is higher, and the department contributes to the number.

- **Customer Service:** The staff is able to move from customer to customer. The Customer Service Manager validated no recent complaints about customer service. There is one piece that is concerning which is the lack of knowledge of competitors. The staff is not aware of competitor pricing, which may be costing the store sales. The managers are educating the staff on the price matching policy, but it is ineffective without some base knowledge of competitive offerings. Competitor shops will be a significant part of the solution plan. Customer complaints have risen in the store, but it is unlikely the automotive department has contributed significantly to that number even with the vacancy.

➢ **Presentation:** The presentation standards were clean and neat. There were a few out of stock items, but they were minimal, and did not disrupt the appearance of the department or perception of an in-stock business. The Department Manager Walk Notes Program was executed and current through last week.

➢ **Replenishment:** The department is restocked well from the replenishing team. They typically have the floor stocked before the store opens. They do not leave any remaining stock for the sales teams. This is a contributor to the customer service success of the department. It allows the sales team to focus on customers and not take their attention away from customers.

➢ **Inventory:** There were no inventory issues noted during the interviews or observations. It is expected that some products will be sold out, but it did not appear to be excessive. There were no reports available to verify the in-stock condition. Inventory will not be included in the solution plan for this area.

- **Receiving:** There were no issues with the receiving process in regards to automotive. The goods were unloaded efficiently and staged for the replenishing team.

Carpet

- **Staffing:** The carpet department had the largest staffing opportunity. The department is short two part-time sales floor associates, and one part time loader. The loader is an individual that assists customers with heavy items to their car. The position also helps to stock the sales floor in the down time. Scott, the Department Manager, stated there were staffing issues last year that were filled this year, this was incorrect. This is the second time a manager was unaware of vacancies.

- **Customer Service:** The layout of the department makes it difficult to view all areas of the department. We did not witness any customer service issues. This would require greater time and review to understand how the vacant positions influence sales. The largest deficit in the department is in stock carpet, which is the hardest to see along the back wall. This area lacks a loader, is there a correlation? The Customer Service Manager validated an issue with signage in the department and pricing.

Customers do not seem to find any issues with the sales team knowledge, but there are new competitors. There was no indication that the team visited or understands the competition.

➢ **Presentation:** There is a primary concern with signage in the department. The racks used can be difficult to sign or for signs to remain in place. The sales person was unsure how the signage should look which is an indicator of an ongoing problem and established norms. There were out of stock carpet rolls in the back wall carpet area. They are noticeable due to the large size of the rolls. There were no reports to indicate how the out of stock condition impacted the sales performance. The Department Manager Walk Notes Program is not completed. The last form completed was four months ago.

➢ **Replenishment:** There were no noticeable issues with larger carpets in the department. There was a stock cart on the floor with area rugs. This cart was being worked on by the salesperson. This cart was in contrast to the comments by Larry, which indicated no problems with getting the department ready for business.

➢ **Inventory:** There were out of stock conditions in the stock carpet roll area. There were no reports available to show the depth or if it is an ongoing problem. There are greater issues in the department, but the stock condition should be noted.

- ➤ **Receiving:** There were no issues with the receiving process noted. There was not a carpet truck being unloaded during the observation. Through interviews, we determined this method is not part of the problem.

Overall Impressions

Contributors: There are several contributors to the problems in the store. There seems to be a lack of managerial presence in all facets of the business.

The issues in the store discovered through reporting and observation led to the following assertions.

- ➲ **Replenish teams do not prioritize the merchandise flow to the sales floor.**

- ➲ **The Department Manager Walk Notes Program is not being completed to react to presentation opportunities such as signage and stock conditions.**

- **Sales associates recognize the lack of managerial presence and become frustrated over the barriers in their jobs. They do not feel managers understand or care about their concerns.**

- **Managers are unaware of their staffing needs. They may not know the staffing matrix.**

- **Managers are altering the staffing standards by relocating associates to other areas, which impacts customer service. This was noted in domestics.**

- **Managers seem to be focused on task and inventory work and not as involved with direct customer contact.**

- **The Store Manager is not coaching, training and developing the management team. Mary is not holding them accountable. She has addressed her concerns but has not followed up on progress.**

- **The Store Manager is not viewing the store as a whole system and has not addressed the sales decline in the largest volume department, carpet.**

There are various contributors to the problem other than managerial issues. The combination of these discoveries contributes to the numerous problems.

⊃ **Sales associates do not discuss the price match policy and do not know competitive offerings.**

⊃ **Company signage standards in the carpeting department, which makes it difficult for the customer shopping experience.**

⊃ **Replenishment team has established norms the influence the flow of goods to the sales floor.**

Gaps: The desired state for the store is becoming clearer through the analysis. The actual state is what has come to light as we compile the data. In the desired state, we want the store to be running an increase and the contributing departments to be progressing effectively and efficiently. This goes beyond the obvious proclamation of a sales increase. Every store team wants to succeed and do well. The desired state in this scenario would have the management team engaged throughout the store.

The managers would be involved in coaching, training and developing both the sales and non-sales teams in the desired state. There would be an emphasis on staffing and educating the management staff of successful retail models. Managers and replenishing teams should be customer focused. Replenishing team should prioritize merchandise flow by sales, staffing and stock condition. They should be trained to replenish the challenging departments. They should be asked about barriers to aid in creating solutions.

There should be an emphasis on consistently completing company programs. If the management staff completed the Department Manager Walk Notes Program, an understanding of stock problems and signage issues may exist. Another issue is taking the competition seriously and reacting to competitive threats in the environment. The central gap that exists in the store is not underperforming departments, rather, underperforming management.

Change: As we continue to process the issues, and the focus shifts from struggling departments to managerial issues, we need to decide what must change. The reason we walk through the steps of this process is to see the bottom of the iceberg. The problems were obvious, a sales decrease. The cause is much more hidden and difficult to define. It is becoming clearer that managers must be immersed in the environment. Their detachment is evident through a lack of understanding barriers and essential needs such as staffing.

What must change is the relationship between Mary and the Assistant Managers in terms of coaching and accountability? The entire team, including Mary, must be aware of their environment through understanding established norms and gathering feedback from their associates. These issues will be addressed in the solutions planning phase. Mary has a real opportunity to improve the environment, and ultimately improve sales performance.

Step 4: Connecting the Whole System

This step may seem redundant, but its intent is a clear picture of the how the problem has impacted the entire store. The reason this step exists is to look beyond the initial problem statement to what must change. What must change is managerial engagement in the store, staffing, competitive intelligence and replenishment prioritization. How will these changes influence the whole system? We will break them down and look at the potential positive and negatives.

Managerial Engagement

- **Managers are currently focused on task work and inventory levels in the store.** If the demand for managers is for more of a sales floor presence, who and how will the inventory process be handled? There needs to be a solution to ensure the in-stock condition does not fall further into disrepair. A managerial presence on the sales floor will help to react to problems that arise such as customer service levels.

- **If managers, including Mary, are educated on managerial**

engagement, how will it occur and what expense will be incurred? The staff needs to be developed, but it may not mean a formal program. Mary may be able to get a handle on accountability and training through organized processes. It is likely that the company will not pay for formal training. Most managers will not admit there are issues with their management style. If we are working with these limitations, how do we get the team to sharpen their skills?

- **Managers that take an associate from domestics and position them somewhere else will create customer service issues.** The domestics department has suffered with customer service due to a lack of help at key times on the floor. This impacts customer overflow from other departments, as well. Why does the team need to pull associates consistently? If there are staffing issues in other departments, they are sacrificing business. The domestics associates are not experts in the departments they are placed, this may diminish the ability to sell in the department.

- **The lack of completing the Department Manager Walk Notes Program has diminished the presentation, signage and inventory in the departments.** This has contributed to the sales decline. What will the process be to ensure this program is completed on a consistent basis?

Staffing

- **There are staffing issues in each of the three departments we observed.** Is it a coincidence that sales performance has declined in these areas? The combined staff deficit in the sales departments and replenishment are six associates. The three sales departments comprise the top three deficits in sales in the store. There are inventory and signage issues in two of the departments.

- **Staffing shortages can impact the ability of surrounding departments during peak times.** The departments are, in a way, interdependent on each other. Typically a neighboring department will assist during peak or overflow times. A staffing shortage can influence more than just the intended department.

Competitive Intelligence

- **The store does not have a working knowledge of the competition.** They do not make visits or educate the selling team on competitive practices. This hinders the ability of the sales team to close sales. If they understood the advantages of the competition, they would be able to overcome them. They need to know the pricing structure of competitors to keep customers in the store and not buying from another retailer.

- **The signage in the carpet department kept customers from understanding the pricing structure and competitive comparisons.** Customers will become frustrated and leave to seek a simpler solution for their needs. This could prevent customers from making future purchases or even buying during the trip to look at carpeting.

- **The competitor may shop the store and create an easy to understand signing system that takes wallet share.** The competitor may have the competitive edge over something as simple as signage.

Replenishment Prioritization

- **The current structure may negatively impact sales by not getting merchandise to departments that depend on a visual presence and in stock condition.** The team does not adhere to the replenishing matrix that directs the soft line areas be replenished first. All departments need inventory to sell, but there has to be a priority when moving goods to the floor.

- **The replenishment process also influences the activity of the sales floor staff when the job is not completed.** This allows carts to be on the floor and takes attention away from customers. A broken replenishment function affects the whole store and customer service.

Step 5: Alternates & Solutions

This is where all of your hard work pays off. You must look through the water and see the deep, dark, larger side of the iceberg. We have narrowed down the problem areas to four interlocking segments. The four segments are managerial engagement, staffing, competitive intelligence and replenishment prioritization. The solution plan will focus on these areas.

Notice that we started this journey with the thought of two departments that were underperforming. We knew there would be underlying causes, but we were not sure how simple or complicated. There are many issues in this scenario, which are easy to repair for long-term growth. There are concerns that involve managers and their abilities to influence employees and be immersed in the business. The managerial issues will not be an easy transition because of the various skill-sets and capabilities. We will be asking managers to analyze their strengths and weaknesses and be willing to work on opportunity areas.

The solution plan requires a reworking of the original problem statement unless it has remained the same. In most cases, the problem statement will change as we discover the scope of the problem. In this retail store scenario, the problem grew from two contributing departments to three with additional elements. The goal of the solution plan is not to surprise your audience with the problem and contributors. This is not a mystery novel. Consultants want to make the issues visible up front. The original problem statement in this case would look like this:

Original problem statement: *A sales decline in the store last year, which has continued, led by two key departments.*

New problem statement: *A sales decline in three key departments that contribute to a store total sales decline of (6%) last year and (2.3%) this year to date. There are four main contributors to the sales decline in the leading departments.*

1. **Managerial Engagement:** A focus on the visibility and understanding of barriers by managers of the key departments.

2. **Staffing:** The staffing shortages that comprise customer service and surrounding departments.

3. **Competitive Intelligence:** The working knowledge and disbursement of knowledge to the sales team of competitor advantages.

4. **Replenishment Prioritization:** The current process inhibits the flow of merchandise to the floor through a lack of adhering to the company guidelines for merchandise processing.

Actual State vs. Desired State

The actual state was determined through interviews, document and policy review, and observations of daily practices.

The Desired State: The Desired State is reversing the sales decline for the total store through recognition and improvement in the four main contributing areas. This state has engaged managers that are proactively removing or reducing barriers to success. Staffing should be 100% complete with employees focused on their role. The staff would have a working knowledge of competitors with an efficient replenishment process.

The Actual State: The actual state finds four major contributors to the sales decline in three significant areas of the store. The discovery phase of this process found opportunities with people, processes and merchandise replenishment that need attention. There is a lack of managerial presence to identify barriers to customer service success. There are staffing needs to meet the company matrix. There is not a current process to understand competitors. Finally, there is a lack of prioritization in replenishing the sales floor, which has created out of stock situations in the examined departments.

Solution Steps

The solution requires a change in the way the key departments of Domestics, Automotive and Carpet are managed. There are similarities in the functional state of these areas as well as unique attributes.

Managerial Engagement

There is a common theme that exists throughout the departments observed. There is a lack of managerial visibility on the sales floor. This includes all layers of management. The lack of managerial presence could be a direct influence on:

- **Staffing turnover in the store is 1.5% higher than last year**
- **Customer complaints in the store increased 2.0% over the last year. Presentation standards in Domestics and Carpet have out of stock and signage issues.**
- **There are replenishment issues in Domestics and Carpet.**
- **There is not a consistent competitive practices program throughout the store.**

To increase managerial presence requires planning. The goal is to increase visibility and accessibility of managers. Managers need to recognize and identify barriers that impede success. This is only possible if they are immersed in the daily life of their people and understand their ideal accomplishments.

1. **Managers must spend a minimum of 50% of their scheduled time on the sales floor with visibility to customers and**

employees. The time invested on the sales floor should be scheduled during peak business times. This should include the three impacted areas and the Store Manager.

2. **Managers of the Domestics, Carpet and Automotive areas, should identify three key barriers to resolve.** The barriers should be determined through observations and interaction with sales floor and replenishment employees.
3. **Managers should thoroughly understand necessary training that needs to be completed for themselves and their people.**
4. **Managers should understand all staffing and sales requirements.**
5. **Assistant Managers must complete the Department Manager Walk Notes Program every two weeks according to policy.** The Store Manager must validate the process is being completed.
6. **Managers must understand the competitors that impact their business** (Action steps are detailed under the Competitive Intelligence section of the solution plan).
7. **The Store Manager must schedule progress meetings with the senior staff monthly.** The meetings should review the current results and develop plans for the upcoming month that consists of key people and merchandise initiatives. The plan should be developed together between the Store Manager and Assistant Manager.

Staffing

There are several inconsistencies that contribute to the shortages in staffing in the three key departments observed. There is not a universal understanding of the staffing matrix. There are opportunities with employee needs and the ability to fill vacant positions. The vacancies cause managers to pull employees to different areas of the store resulting in coverage shortages and a decline in customer service. The vacant positions are influencing sales results through the following indicators.

- **Staffing turnover in the store is 1.5% higher than last year.**
- **Customer complaints in the store increased 2.0% over the last year.**
- **Presentation standards in Domestics and Carpet have out of stock and signage issues.**

The current vacancies in the key contributing departments and supporting functions include: 2 full time and 5 part time positions. This has resulted in customers that are not assisted and eventually leave the department. The shortage also influences the replenishment process. This creates a need for the sales staff to invest time into stocking shelves, as opposed to assisting customers. The following plan is to achieve company set staffing standards.

1. **Each member of the senior staff must receive a copy of the staffing matrix within three business days.**
2. **The open positions should be posted through the HR**

Department following the company-approved guideline.

3. **Managers must consider a whole system view before they adjust staffing in departments or position an employee in another department.**

4. **Managers should update employees of their plan to fill the staffing matrix.** This may reduce frustration of current employees that are working harder to compensate for the lack of staffing.

5. **Managers should invest more of their scheduled time in departments that are short staffed.** This will ensure customer service standards are maintained.

6. **The managers must have a mid afternoon meeting daily for 15 minutes.** The Store Manager must be present during scheduled days. The purpose of the meeting is to review the daily tasks required and special projects, as well. This educates the managers as a unified staff that connects all of the areas together to reach goals.

Competitive Intelligence

There are opportunities to understand the competition at a deep level to enable the store to be proactive to customer needs and trends. Managers need to understand their competitive advantages and disadvantages to enable the store to react. There is currently not a consistent program to capture competitive information and disseminate it to the sales team. The lack of a competitive program is validated through lost sales and the following:

- **Customer complaints in the store increased 2.0% over the last year.**

There are a few things to consider when addressing competitor intelligence. This goes beyond the advertised product or product selection. Managers must consider the competitor through the entire experience including customer service, sales team knowledge, products, pricing and programs. Once the information is gathered, the employees need to understand how to use the knowledge to increase sales.

1. **The team should review, print and distribute to employees any price matching policies that exist.** The goal is to educate the team to keep customers in the store from going to competitors.
2. **Managers should create a list of competitors that influence their business within a five mile radius.** The list will be used to develop a competitive shop program.
3. **The next step is to create a schedule for managers and key employees to visit primary competitors every thirty days.** Stagger the visits to ensure information is current and relevant in the market.
4. **The competitive visits should be focused and defined before they occur.** The manager or employee should focus on products and services that are available in their department to enable them to be experts.

5. **There should be competitive shop binders in every department that consists of the most recent shop and current pricing.** This will enable the team to be proactive to competitive programs and pricing.

Replenishment Prioritization

The opportunities that exist in replenishment involve oversight and direction of the process. There is a company derived plan for merchandise flow. The Replenishment Team makes the decision to move product based on personal understanding and ease of product flow. The result is a misaligned flow that leaves additional product on the floor in more challenging departments such as Domestics. The sales team has to complete the process, which takes the focus from customer service. The lack of prioritization has influenced the following.

- **Staffing turnover in the store is 1.5% higher than last year.**
- **Customer complaints in the store increased 2.0% over the last year.**
- **Presentation standards in Domestics and Carpet have out of stock and signage issues.**
- **There are replenishment issues in Domestics and Carpet.**

The team, according to the company guidelines, is led by the Administrative Manager in the store. The following suggestions include direct oversight by their immediate supervisor to ensure prioritization. The Store Manager should verify the implementation and effectiveness of the solution plan.

1. **The team needs to be staffed according to the company matrix.**
2. **The team must be current with all company training.**
3. **The company merchandise flow guidelines, should be printed and discussed with the Replenishment Team.** The Administrative Manager should work with the team for the first week to lead by example for the process.
4. **The process should be reviewed and validated monthly through feedback from Assistant Managers and sales floor employees.**
5. **Merchandise that cannot be stocked before the replenishment shift ends must be planned on the sales floor.** There must be a time established for all merchandise carts to leave the sales floor. The carts should be removed prior to peak business times. This will keep the sales team focused on customer service.

Time Line and Roles

The proposed changes should begin immediately following a discussion with the senior staff. It is essential for the success of any plan to schedule implementation and accountability. There needs to be a meeting scheduled to discuss the scope of change.

The initial meeting will set the stage for change and assign roles. The following is a schedule of times and individuals accountable for parts of the plan.

General Meeting - July 1.

Managerial Engagement - Begins July 1, Accountable: Store Manager, Domestic Manager, Automotive Manager, Carpet Manager.

Staffing – Begins July 1, job postings should be ready by July 3, jobs filled by August 1. Monthly reviews scheduled the first Tuesday of every month. Accountable: Store Manager, Domestic Manager, Automotive Manager, Carpet Manager.

Competitive Intelligence – Begins July 1, schedules for competitive shops should be completed the first of every month. Accountable: Store Manager, Domestic Manager, Automotive Manager, Carpet Manager.

Replenishment Prioritization – Begins July 1, job postings should be ready by July 3 and jobs filled by August 1. Administrative Manager will meet and discuss the company flow by July 3. The Administrative Manager will work the same schedule as the team the first week of August.

Milestones and Checkpoints

There will be monthly meetings or specific time in scheduled meetings dedicated to the Solution Plan. The accountable members should give an update for their area of responsibility and discuss the following.

- **Progress towards the desired state**
- **Barriers & Solutions**
- **Adjustments that may be required**
- **Wins and opportunities**

These topics should be discussed as a team and solutions should be considered as a group. The required attendees must be the Store Manager/ Domestic Manager/ Automotive Manager/ Carpet Manager and Administrative Manager.

Gauge Success

The success of the proposed changes hinges upon the inclusion of diverse views and feedback from the group. The Store Manager cannot solely determine the success or failure of a component of change. The group should consist of the following.

- **Store Manager**

- **Domestics Manager**
- **Automotive Manager**
- **Carpet Manager**
- **Receiving Manager**
- **Administrative Manager**
- **1 Domestics employee**
- **1 Automotive employee**
- **1 Carpet employee**
- **1 Replenishment employee**
- **Customer Service Manager**

The list may seem extensive. Differing views are needed to determine the ongoing effectiveness of the plan. The list can be reduced if there are signs of consistent improvement.

The following reports and programs should be utilized to analyze success or the need for adjustments.

- **Sales Reports**
- **Staffing Reports**
- **Product Line Reports**
- **Department Manager Walk Notes Program**
- **Turnover Ratio Reports**
- **Customer Complaint Reports**

In addition to these measures, managers should schedule observations to ensure customer service has improved and employee morale has increased. The culmination of these measures will complete a picture from the store side. Customers should be asked a few brief questions during management's dedicated floor time. The point is not to inconvenience the customer, rather, gather information on the most important piece to this puzzle, the customer experience.

The suggested questions are:

- **How was your shopping experience today on a scale of 1 to 5? (1 being not good and 5 being excellent)**
- **What could we have done better for you today?**
- **Are there any questions or additional assistance needed?**

These questions will help managers gain insight into what the customer is thinking. It is essential that a manager greet customers through a personal introduction to show a heightened sense of interest in the customer response. The Store Manager should schedule time for customer reviews, as well.

CHAPTER 6

UNDERCURRENTS IN THE ENVIRONMENT

How do hiring practices in your organization relate to retail consulting? When it comes to the development and morale of the staff, the methods that are used are critical. Many highly visible problems that exist in the store are linked to a breakdown in the development of people. Take this thought further to how people are promoted and if they possess the capability to succeed. A Retail Consultant may look at why the staffing structure is in place and what employees receive to learn and grow. This is necessary to resolve current issues related to development and for future planning.

Part of seeing your business from a consultative perspective is reviewing how your store promotes and develops managers. The practices currently used influence the culture in the store. When Store Managers are considering potential influences on the morale of the store, they must evaluate how the staff leads and develops. They should also review how people are trained and promoted.

So much of your focus is on product and processes. The underlying issues may go further to include a morale problem in the store. Morale will influence productivity and customer service in the store. The hard part about people issues is identifying them readily and attributing them to a visible problem. It is easy to see the end-result of a problem such as declined sales or customer service scores. You must figure out how the store reached the level of decline and what lies under the current.

The case study revealed elements lacking in coaching, training and development by the staff. This must be considered when dissecting a problem. The best-case scenario is changing your mindset now to influence the future positively. This includes changing the way you evaluate candidates to move into management or further into management.

Undercurrents

The opportunity to work with a retail consultant at the store level does not occur often. It is an expense, and in a retail chain it is less likely. The purpose of this book is to give you the tools to look at your business objectively. You must learn to see things through the eyes of your customer and without bias. This will bring managers closer to creating lasting solutions to problems.

Retail consultants train and use their expertise in diverse situations. Think about your store and the complex scenarios that arise in relation to variables. Store Managers may not be an expert in different types of retail, but they can become the expert of their business. The key is developing disciplines that deepen your understanding of the store and its people. Consider what makes the store tick and what influences the performance both good and bad.

A good place to start understanding what makes the store function is the environment. You need to have a deep level view of the undercurrents that influence the culture in the store. An area to examine is how people learn and grow. You cannot expect the environment to move forward if there is no plan for coaching, training and developing the team.

Store Managers should be tapped into the undercurrents of the culture. There has to be a structure for learning. Learning occurs throughout three levels. The first is through senior managers in the store. The second level is through Department Managers or entry level management. The third is through the employee base. The reason they are in this order is the path of learning. Your senior level managers are accountable for developing the entry level team. The Department Managers are closer to integral components of the business, the sales floor team and customers.

You cannot overlook the connection to results by Department Managers. They are typically involved in the daily routine of employees, and they are the front line for customers. They are also left to sink or swim on their own. They learn to interact with people and lead them through observation and instinct. This leaves a tremendous amount of room for interpretation and motivation of the team towards the same goals.

The undercurrent does not appear in a quick fashion, rather, they are practices that develop slowly over time. The foundation and basis of your team morale is placed upon a management staff's ability to promote and cultivate talent. This is an area that is often painful for managers to look at because there is a personal failure involved with a struggling morale. When you are analyzing problems, consider how the team got there and where your methods may contribute to the issue.

The purpose is to begin thinking and changing your perspective now to reduce problems in the future. This should be considered a proactive measure to develop and strengthen a staff. Retail Consultants will analyze your practices to understand problems with morale. The good news, you do not need to wait for a problem to arise. You can begin building a better staff today.

How Managers are Promoted

HR Managers usually create and enforce hiring policies that align with legal and state requirements. The policies are typically enforced by your organization. They ensure the work environment is fair and equitable. The structure is necessary to enable individuals to have an ethical opportunity for job placement and promotion. It also offers managers a guideline to follow to be consistent from store to store.

The policies are a necessary component of a retail business. They structure the approach, but policies do not make the final decision. The Store or Assistant Manager, in most retailers, give the final approval to fill a position. How do you determine who should fill a role or promotion?

The ability of a manager to evaluate a potential candidate for promotion is handed down through a rushed and incomplete process. This hand-me-down knowledge perpetuates the placement of under qualified individuals into managerial roles. You are left with a store that has a mediocre staff that works harder but accomplishes less.

The launching point for most retail managerial careers is the Department Manager position. This is the training ground to advance further into leadership roles with the company. The decision to promote an individual is often pre-determined before the interview process. You already know whom you like and may be a good fit. The interview process may sway your decision to another candidate, but more than likely you go with your gut choice. While it is a good practice to be thinking ahead for talent to fill roles, the process is often skewed.

Think about your Department Manager team in the store. Which qualifiers do you use to determine Department Manager skill sets? How does their abilities align with managing people? Typically, the decision to promote an employee to manager is based on performance in their current role. You may have a top tier salesperson that breaks all of the records, but does that mean they are capable of leading people. If your decision to promote a person is based on an impressive performance, you are feeling your way through the dark. Will this person succeed, no one knows, but you should take a closer look at the ability of the person to lead.

The decision to promote into management can also be erroneously based on popularity or political considerations. Maybe the individual has worked for the company for a long time or aligns with your decision-making on everything. These are not true indicators of leadership. You need to be surrounded with the best people. This will increase your chances of success. The greater chance of success lies in making intelligent decisions about managerial promotions.

The current performance of a candidate should be considered in the evaluation of their abilities, but it should not be the sole identifier. Of course, you want to place an individual that has signs of success in their current role. If they are currently failing, they need additional training and resources before they should be considered further. Take into consideration all of the factors that drive success for a candidate. Their area may be experiencing a surge in business. There may be additional advertising efforts or inventory surpluses that influence results.

The same consideration should be given to higher-level promotions, as well. How do you determine which Department Managers should be promoted into higher roles, such as Assistant Manager? The same methods are typically used to promote into these positions. The Store Manager bases the ability of a Department Manager to lead solely on their current numerical and visual performance. If the manager has solid numbers and the area looks good, Store Managers assume the individual must be ready to motivate a larger mass of people.

A Retail Consultant may determine selection practices are a part of the problem with people related issues in the store. You are the retail consultant in your store. You need to view these practices as a part of a problem or solution. If you currently select individuals based mainly on the factors mentioned, you are creating problems down the road for the store. You can break the cycle now and become a better evaluator of talent. This does not require a special class or certification. This requires an ability to view your business and practices objectively.

If your store has been properly staffed, the hiring and promotion practices should be examined. You need to develop your Assistant Managers to consider candidates in the same way. They are often involved with promoting Department Managers or sales people into elevated positions. In my last book, there is a quick set of questions to gain a further understanding of a candidate. These questions apply to all levels of management. The intent of the questions is to look beyond surface performance. This will uncover the true potential that lies within the candidate.

- **Can you identify leadership qualities from the individual's current performance?**
- **Can you identify any barriers or obstacles the individual has overcome to succeed?**
- **Have you witnessed the results of creative or innovative ideas the individual has demonstrated to succeed?**
- **Have you witnessed customer interaction with this person?**
- **Have you witnessed employee interaction with this person?**
- **What influence has this person had on the success of the department & store?**
- **Does this individual's talent align with the company's vision?**
- **What do you really know about this person through personal interaction?**

- Has the individual shown openness for change?
- Does this person have the ability and capability to balance accountability and relationships with people?
- What established norms, both good & bad, have you witnessed with this individual?

Employees and lower level managers should be promoted based on performance and ability to connect and lead people. You are looking for an individual that can balance connecting with people and accountability. The individual should be ready today to move forward. You should not place an individual in a managerial role that still needs time to develop. You need to give an individual the greatest chance of success as opposed to placing them before they are ready.

Managers or employees are expected to mature into their position through growth and learning. They must be receptive to learning and developing in their role before moving forward. Too often, a need arises, and the decision is made to rush an individual through channels. This will create a development opportunity and a sink or swim mentality. Often an individual will continue to be pushed through channels only to fail at a much higher or greater level.

Managing people is a balancing act learned through experience and development. No one is expected to be an expert upon entering the profession. The expectation is a level of maturity in their current role and the capability of growth in the next role. Once the decision is made to promote an individual, the accountability for managers in the store does not end. The environment must continue to foster growth for individuals to develop in their roles.

Managerial Development

Developing managers is an ongoing process of enhancing their skill-set and capabilities. The goal of developing managers is to leverage your strengths on staff and limit the weaknesses. Everyone needs continuous development in their role to grow, and become more effective. Learning should never cease and should be an accepted part of the culture. This requires an intimate knowledge of the environment including the norms established by managers.

Store Managers have a tricky job. They need to ensure Department Managers are receiving the guidance they need and develop Assistant Managers. The Assistant Managers must be developed in their roles and trained to develop Department Managers. It is a cycle of learning and teaching. The Department Managers learn and coach the employee base. No matter the role, there is a constant state of connecting with people and development. To enable you to begin developing the team, you need to know the following.

- The strengths and weaknesses of the managers.
- Identify learning and growth opportunities.
- Understand their ability to learn.
- The individual's future aspirations.

If there are weaknesses in morale and the store culture, a Retail Consultant may examine the learning environment. You need to step back and evaluate the stores' learning environment. Part of the process is reviewing performances in the store. You cannot manage or base decisions solely upon numerical performance. It can indicate an issue or validate success. The main ingredient is a personal interest and relationship with your staff. This means you have to care that the staff is continually learning. It must be relevant to you to become essential to the environment.

A learning environment has an upside for the store. It reduces turnover, encourages loyalty and keeps the team on track as a unit working towards the company vision. It ultimately equates to a high performance team that cares about the work they perform. The team can depend on learning about their role and where it fits in the big picture. It makes them feel like more than a number which will inspire a harder determination and drive within them.

The two views to consider are reactive and proactive.

- **How do you proactively foster a learning environment?**

⮂ **How do you recognize opportunities in the store environment?**

Identifying an opportunity within your environment for learning is not difficult. It requires a connection with people and involvement with daily functions. You need to be close to people to get feedback from them. The place to start is with employees and Department Managers. They are the closest to the customer and create results.

This can be accomplished in short, simple conversations during your rounds throughout the building. What involvement does your Assistant Managers have with developing their managers? You need to ask Department Managers if they have the ongoing tools to succeed. Ask for one barrier that prohibits success and follow up with how they have been helped to remove it. You should talk about their last performance review and if their opportunities and aspirations were discussed. It may sound generic, but a few questions will grant insight into the current learning environment at the base level.

The next step is scheduling time with your Assistant Managers. This time is to assess the current status of developing people and their potential. This requires a structured approach to ensure an understanding of their abilities. The goal is assessing where their opportunities lie and begin the coaching process to identify opportunities in managers.

There needs to be a developmental plan created between the Store and Assistant Manager that addresses opportunity areas. A component of the plan relies upon your observations of the area. The plan cannot rely solely upon numerical performance. This is where the conversations with Department Managers and employees contribute to the development of the plan. The areas should be chosen after reviewing all of the components that comprise the manager's area of responsibility, personal assessment and your observations.

The Assistant Manager should personally assess their performance. This is often difficult for most to do. It is hard to see your opportunities as clearly as others may. The collaborative effort between the Store Manager and Assistant is vital in constructing the plan. A personal assessment should include areas such as:

- **Customer service**
- **Employee development**
- **Follow up/ Feedback to employees**
- **Delegation**
- **Planning**
- **Succession planning**
- **Problem solving/ Solutions**
- **Competitive Intelligence**

The Assistant Manager should evaluate theses areas to determine strengths and weaknesses. The plan will start to take shape as opportunity areas should include a personal assessment entry, a Store Manager observational entry and another that comes from the discussion. The meeting and development plan are a proactive way to ensure development and promote ongoing learning. The meeting should be held with each Assistant Manager separately with ample time to create the plan. Here are some general guidelines for a constructive meeting.

- **Create an agenda for the meeting and send it out a week in advance to stimulate thought around topics. Also, send the assessment for the manager to come prepared.**
- **Discuss your observations of the manager's area in a constructive way.**
- **Discuss the results of the personal assessment.**
- **Create an action plan for development.**
- **Set deadlines and timelines within the plan.**
- **Set follow up meeting dates and times.**
- **Ask for a commitment to the process to promote growth and development.**

This is not a one shot deal. A proactive plan is an ongoing, living, breathing document. The plan is an ongoing process of improvement that will change as an area is improved. There will also be areas uncovered that need addressed or added in the future.

The development of managers should be a part of your review process and considered when evaluating the store environment. A Retail Consultant would dig into development practices for the store and potentially add actions to the improvement plan.

Employee Development

Employee development is no less significant than managerial development. The reason we discussed managerial development first is managers directly influence the environment. A lack of employee development will directly affect the bottom line. Employees are on the front lines, and if managers limit their ability to learn and grow, they are limiting the ability of the store and sales to grow.

If the store is experiencing problems in morale or turnover, a Retail Consultant will review your hiring practices and the ongoing experiences for your employees. This area requires proactive measures. You need to establish methods now as opposed to waiting for a problem. Think about the amount of time and expense it takes to hire one individual. Consider the amount of business that may be sacrificed through losing their experience. It is beneficial for your store to create plans now to develop people and be your own consultant.

There are collective experiences in the environment that indicate a closed environment. The indicators are hard to see at times because of the various abilities and personalities of the managers. There may be a more skilled manager that connects with their team in one area while another lacks the people connection. You may begin to notice an issue when sales decline in an area. This usually will begin the investigative process.

The indicators will generally include a sales decline, higher turnover, lack of productivity, high absenteeism, declining customer service scores, a rise in customer complaints and low morale. It may not be everything at once, but it is typically a combination of some of these elements. These experiences are in direct correlation to a lack of growth and connection with people. Your people feel unappreciated, and they will not commit to your efforts or the company. You have to give to get, when it comes to people.

Morale has to be in good shape or on its way to being repaired before true learning can take place. A solid morale is in direct correlation with the ability of managers to connect with people. If your people feel good about what they do, they will want to work harder. Developing your team instills loyalty and trust. They will apply their learning to driving sales and increasing profits.

There are two layers of management that directly influence the morale and development of employees. The Department Manager, in many retailers, is the immediate supervisor of the employee team. They may make the schedule, delegate workloads, provide ongoing training, assist with customer service issues and provide input with disciplinary measures, promotions or terminations. The Assistant Manager will typically execute terminations and disciplines. They will oversee the larger operation and may be involved in daily decisions of the area. The combination of these positions account for the connection of an employee to the company.

The ability of the two layers of managers in developing employees is essential because Store Managers cannot improve everyone in the building. It is critical that Store Managers invest in developing their direct reports in the area of employee relations and development. This requires Assistant and Department Managers to simultaneously develop their people while working on their own personal growth. This is where your guidance as a Store Manager is essential to balance their learning while coaching them to teach others.

Developing employees requires a structured approach to ensure consistency. You must follow a structure that takes into account the various skills and capabilities of the Assistant and Department Managers. The structure should be simple and thorough to ensure there is a good understanding of the development areas for an employee. Managers need to invest time into a discussion that clarifies the employee's role, offers insight into where the role fits in the organization, offers ongoing assistance to remove barriers and defines a career path. The Store Managers role is to guide the relationship and ensure the team is receiving the necessary coaching through validation.

The following are suggestions for beginning the development process. These actions are not overnight singular conversations. This requires frequent and ongoing interaction and connecting.

- **Ensure employees understand the value in the work they perform daily.** This is accomplished through two avenues. The first is through daily interactions during the course of the day. Tie the value they represent into milestones and wins. The second is through performance evaluations. The performance evaluation should tie the work performed to future aspirations.

- **Recognize employee accomplishments that align with the company vision.** The company has a vision statement that encapsulates its values and mission. The vision is the gauge for all productive activity in the store. The management staff must unify the team to work towards the vision or common goal. Morale hinges upon recognition of wins and ties them into the vision. You need to have a good morale in the store for employees to be receptive to a learning environment. Employee recognition reinforces morale and a learning environment. Managers should publically recognize employees for wins to share them with the store.

- **Consistent coaching of employees to develop skills.** Coaching is a daily event that offers employees guidance that aligns with the vision. Coaching is an act that contributes to the knowledge base of the employee. Coaching enhances the skills of an individual by offering a different perspective to customer service and productivity. Coaching should occur during the daily course of work and be proactive in nature. This should not be disciplinary or negative. Those issues should be held separately and in a private setting. Store Managers should coach employees in a general nature. The Assistant and Department Managers should perform the more intensive coaching. These managers are the primary influence of change, and they are directly involved with performance plans.

- **Define employee roles and responsibilities.** Employees need to have a fundamental understanding of their role. They need to understand how their role fits into the big picture of the store and company. Accountability is a significant part of development. Accountability is an understanding of expectations and consequences. Defining the combination of roles and responsibilities for an employee makes their contribution easier to connect with success. They understand the expectations, feel supported and they are receptive to a learning environment.

Retail consulting should turn over every rock to find the cause of a problem. The undercurrents are a little more difficult to identify when it comes to people. There are many variables to consider that comprise the work ethic and attitudes of employees. They are not as easy to figure out as inventory issues or trends. People must be a part of your thought process for strengthening or repairing your store. If stores have an open, learning environment, it will promote a more productive environment.

CHAPTER 7

THE BROKEN BUILDING ENVIRONMENT

A broken building has many different failures occurring at the same time. The failures require an organized plan to begin repairing the environment. It is difficult to begin with a solution strategy in this environment. Store Managers need to get the basics together before extensive planning will be effective. In a broken building, there are many issues at the surface that lead to various sources of the problems. It is like, skipping a stone across the water and watching the ripples that begin small and eventually spread. The problem begins in one area and spreads to other areas of the business. Even after the stone stops, the ripples continue to move the unsettled water.

A broken building has several issues that range across the business identifiers. Morale is typically low. It is impacted by other key components. The problems are visible throughout many of the identifiers. It is challenging to get a handle on the multiple sources that are lurking at the heart of the issues. Before we continue, let's look back at the six main identifiers that were discussed in Chapter 3.

1. **Business Performance (Numerical Data)**
2. **Customers**
3. **Employees/ Environment**
4. **Presentation/ Assortment**
5. **Competition**
6. **Processes**

The identifiers are accepted barometers of health for a retail unit. They are broad in nature to cover a vast amount of activities. If you understand the identifiers under this umbrella, you will typically be able to recognize problems that exist within the structure. The reason the identifiers are beneficial in broken buildings is recognition of the various problems. Since the building has already suffered due to a network of broken variables, the identifiers expose the problems for Store Managers.

The identifiers are launching points to unravel the actual source of the problem. There are three basics to understand for getting the most out of identifiers. This includes what the identifier currently represents. This also includes how managers can leverage what the identifier is trying to express. The three points to consider are:

1. **The problem is already at the surface, which means it has been developing.**
2. **The identifiers only represent the surface issues.**
3. **The identifiers are viewed independently. They should be viewed as a part of the whole system.**

The problem is already at the surface, which means it has been developing. This is the more obvious of the basics mentioned. The reason a broken building is easy to identify is the alarming numbers of red flags that exist within the identifiers. The identifiers recognize the problem after it exists. This means the problem has been developing under the surface for some time. In some cases, such as established norms, it could be years. This allows managers to work backwards to find out how the problem began and how the problem connects to other areas. It may give insight into other areas the problem has influenced.

The identifiers only represent the surface issues. This is the launching point to investigate the cause of the problem. This point intertwines with the first one, and the problem being at the surface. The identifier represents the result of the story, but it does not tell the story. The problem that has risen to the surface is the result of many other elements at work. The undercurrents contribute to developing problems. What you see at the surface is not the only consideration for creating solutions. If you are creating solutions for the surface issue, you are treating the symptom and not the cause. The bandage that is applied to the situation will never work for the long term.

The identifiers are viewed independently. They should be viewed as a part of the whole system. When Store Managers are looking beneath the surface at the origination of a problem, they may find a tangled web of other issues blocking the view. Rarely does a problem take a straight path and only affect one area of the business. There are usually several elements that are working together to bring the issue to the surface. The whole system is the entire environment. We discussed the whole system view in Chapter 2 to include customers, employees, resources, expenses, policies, areas that surround the problem or interest, competition, as well as merchandising and brands. The whole system is everything that is influenced or will be influenced by a decision, change or problem.

Think of the whole system as the inner workings of a clock. All of the gears are designed to work together to make the clock function accurately. If there is a problem with one gear, it directly influences another gear and the clock no longer accurately keeps time. When you look behind the face of the problem, you may see several gears that are no longer working. The advantage to considering the whole system is an understanding of how the problem is influencing or creating other problems.

If you view the problems as independent issues, you may never get to the cause of the problem. You may never identify other areas that need addressed through a singular lens. You need to look at the problems and the interconnectivity to other matters. This will gain insight into the scope of the issues. Considering the whole system is vital for problem solving which is step 4 of the retail consulting principles.

Retail Consultant & the Broken Store

Where does a Retail Consultant fit into a broken store environment? The consultant does not enter the building with assumptions. They have to begin the assignment with an inquisitive mind and begin the discovery process. They need to know where the building needs to be, the goals and vision. The task may be monumental, but they follow the consulting principles and organize the information to create solutions.

You are the Retail Consultant in the store. You cannot let assumptions skew your approach. It is ok to know that failures exist. You should reflect on past solutions to learn about the environment. It is not a good idea to go into the environment with a plan for change before you have the chance of evaluating the surroundings.

The ability to understand the environment requires a prioritization of the issues to tackle the largest causes first. It also takes patience to untangle the issues, and create whole system solutions. This is where your practice and discipline becomes valuable. Store Managers are a Retail Consultant when they enter the store. They evaluate the identifiers from an unbiased perspective. You should not be attached to the staff and established norms. You are basing the effectiveness of the operation from a learning perspective. You are looking for the good and the bad to leverage both in the planning. You are basing the resolution on what is best for the business.

You cannot tackle extensive solution planning until you begin to repair the environment. If you try to create large scale, complex changes in a building where the basics of people, processes and presentation are not healthy, the planning will fail. An assessment of the environment to identify the scope of the issues is necessary before repairing the culture can begin.

Assessing the Environment

Managers often fear the dreaded broken building assignment. Some managers look at the many obstacles and low morale as a challenge. Regardless of which side you fall on, this assignment is a great opportunity. The challenge is to balance an unstable culture that requires considerable time to repair. The good news is the environment can be fixed. The repair requires an organized plan, and the capability to connect with people.

A broken building is a result of poor leadership and a disconnect with people. Some broken buildings are obvious to the naked eye through numerous reporting issues at the surface. The broken store is the one in the district that ranks the worst at everything. Sales may have suffered, and processes typically lack execution. Employee turnover may be high, and morale is low. Productivity has slowed, and building conditions have declined. When you look at all of these issues, it becomes an obvious case of deficient leadership.

There are some broken buildings that are less obvious to the naked eye. This type of store usually flies under the radar. The problems may exist more on the employee side of the business. Morale and people issues are much more difficult to identify than sales problems. The store may be doing well in a numerical sense, but the people and productivity issues are preventing the store from reaching its full potential.

There is a difference between these two types of broken buildings. First, you may know what you are walking into with an obvious situation. Second, you will not realize the issues immediately. As you move around and accept challenges that lie within the company, the chance of being placed in a broken building is fairly good. The first thing that needs to happen is an assessment of the environment.

Regardless of the current condition of the store, you need to assess the environment before you change anything. Even in obvious broken buildings, how do you know what to change or the cause unless you have evaluated the environment? Even if all of the issues are transparent, you cannot begin managing the building based on assumptions. You may believe that the store has many unproductive people and begin terminating employees only to find out they were never coached, trained or developed to succeed.

Store Managers need to assess their surroundings through evaluation and observation. This goes beyond shuffling through a stack of reports to being immersed in the environment. You cannot pass judgment until you have a firm understanding of where the breakdowns are occurring. You need to utilize the business identifiers before you begin creating solutions.

Keep in mind that different buildings may require a different approach. You may have fixed buildings in your last few assignments, but that does not guarantee that same pattern will work. That is why assessment is so essential. For example, you may have handled the last two assignments with a tough, less people centric focus and turned the building around. On this assignment, people may not be receptive, and the previous strategy may fail.

The assessment should be organized by grouping the identifiers into three segments to begin the process.

1. **Business Performance/ Competition**
2. **Customers/ Employees & Environment**
3. **Presentation/ Processes**

This allows for a closely related discovery process without being overwhelmed with six separate identifiers. The identifiers are linked, and one will generally influence the other. For example, if employees are not trained, customer service will suffer. If your business performance has declined, the competition will become more of a factor. If the presentation standards have slipped, there are processes that are not being executed. You will dig deeper into the individual components, and how they influence each other, but you need to have an organized starting point. Here are some tips for the assessment process.

- **Begin with reporting and competition.** You need to have a fundamental understanding of where issues may reside. Depending on the state of the broken building, issues may be obvious or hidden. Take note of areas that are currently trending down to provide an additional emphasis on observation in those areas. The reporting should act as a guide through the store. It will not tell the story, only give the results. You should also know whom the competitors are in the area. This will help as you begin discussions with employees in areas that have declined.

- **Connect with Customers and Employees in the environment.** This is where the story is told, through the eyes of customers and employees. The reason managers do not start the assessment with people is they need a general sense of where obvious failures are occurring. This understanding molds your questions and investigation around the details. If you understand the facts and trouble spots in the store, you can look for clues throughout the introductory walk of the store. You should spend as much time as you can on the floor talking with people. This is a learning phase. You should not begin change or talk about how you believe the store got to this point. The conversation should be around development, growth and a future that aligns with the company's vision. Listen to the feedback from customers and employees and their thoughts on the environment. You can also observe the level of interaction of employees with customers.

- **End with presentation and processes.** As you walk through the store, you will notice the conditions and presentation practices. These areas may correlate with your earlier review of the reporting. You may notice a decline in sporting goods sales and note that the presentation has several out of stock issues. You may also notice several carts of new goods waiting to reach the shelves still sitting in the receiving area because of a broken process.

The goal is to experience the environment through the eyes of a customer. That is how a Retail Consultant would view your environment. If a store is not performing well in an area, what does the customer see? If there is an issue, what lies beneath the surface that is creating the problem. You want to emerge from your initial observation with an idea of where further investigation is needed. You also want to gather a sense of the last Store Managers connection with people. If an issue exists with developing people, it probably accounts for many of the undercurrents that exist.

Repairing the Environment

Repairing the environment is a tough but rewarding road. It is not enough to just fix the problems that exist. The surface and undercurrents need long-term solutions to return the function to a healthy state. There are three categories to consider in your rebuilding process for long-term change. The categories consist of people, presentation and processes. The three categories represent the most influential elements to repairing an environment. These factors are the foundation for healing the culture in the broken building and starting the recovery process. If you get these areas on the way to recovery, you can begin to take a deeper dive into problems and create solution plans.

There are many questions as you begin the long road to recovery. The discoveries will ultimately lead to more questions that need to be answered. Repairing your environment with a focus on the three categories of people, presentation and processes allows you to begin rebuilding the three areas at one time. The rebuilding processes will occur at three levels, but they will not overwhelm your team. If you throw too many major changes at employees, they may drown in all of the activity. They cannot keep up with complexity and loss of comfort that change brings. It disrupts the established norms and forces them to think and act differently.

The changes that you implement around people, presentation and processes align with the company's vision. The changes are not a drastic departure, rather, a return to where the environment should have already been. Employees may welcome the change in basics to return to a balanced workplace. You are not looking to create a new environment or make new rules. The goal is to connect with people, ensure presentation standards are consistent and improve processes.

Presentation

The presentation piece of the building is usually the place most Store Managers begin. It is the path of least resistance, and there are typically guidelines already established by the company. It is also the best way for employees to begin seeing and feeling change. If the presentation is broken in many places, the change will be quick and noticeable. If the building presentation is in good shape, there may be tweaking, and there is an opportunity to remain consistent.

You need to conduct a presentation review to determine the state of the store. This may consist of merely walking the floor and taking observational notes to walking with company guide materials such as plan-o-grams. Store Managers do not have time to walk every plan in the store. The goal is to check a few to gauge the level of attention paid to presentation. You need to walk the store through the eyes of the customer. You must pay attention to promotional spaces and in line presentations.

You need to organize your efforts for a few reasons. First, there will be simultaneous change occurring in other elements, in the store. Second, you want to begin establishing expectations for the long-term. Presentation standards should be established and then enforced. There are so many moving parts and elements in the store. Presentation should be a daily, instilled work ethic. Here are a few suggestions for establishing initial presentation standards.

- **Review company programs that address presentation.** Most large retail chains have standards in print to give the store management team direction. This is great information to review before you begin the sales floor walk. There may also be standards to review on in-stock or full shelf standards. You may notice presentation standards during the walk that do not align with company standards, and the areas should be noted. If the documents can be printed, carry them on the walk. If there are no printed guidelines, review any materials that pertain to the visual, and in-stock aspect of the store before the floor walk.

- **Complete an initial walk of the sales floor.** This requires nothing but a small notepad to make notes, and viewing the floor through the eyes of a customer. You should note any presentations that lack structure, has empty spaces or looks disorganized. This is not designed to take days to complete. This should take a few hours during your normal rounds on the floor. The purpose is to give your upcoming meeting structure, and offer you a customer's perspective. You are not looking to give direction during the walk, rather, purely observe the current conditions.

- **Schedule a meeting with Assistant and Department Managers to discuss expectations.** The focus of the meeting is reintroducing the presentation standards in the store and setting the expectations. You want both layers of management present to ensure they both hear the expectations from you and can start repairing the presentation standards in the store without delay. The meeting should be an inspirational message about change. The message is getting back to the basics. If there are printed materials, they should be distributed to ensure consistency. The meeting should discuss the current state and the desired state in a factual sense. You do not need to be negative to drive home the point. You want to move forward as a team. Regardless of the last Store Managers style and beliefs, moving forward means moving from the past. This is a great opportunity to connect with the team. Ensure to designate timelines to follow up with the team. The managers need to understand that presentation is a daily situation and not a project. The meetings should be quick and to the point. You want to get the team back to work with a willingness to work hard.

- **Discuss presentation standards at daily meetings.** In many big box retailers, there are daily meetings that are held for the morning, afternoon or evening shifts. These meetings are sometimes-called huddles. The meetings are typically held on the sales floor. The goal is to get through them quickly and still be visible on the floor. The purpose of the meeting is disseminating information throughout various shifts. This is an excellent opportunity to discuss the presentation standards for consistency. You can have the meeting in an area of the store that exemplifies presentation standards. You do not want to have the meeting in a poorly presented area. It embarrasses people and may be counterproductive to your cause. The message should be about executing the basics and how that influences customer buying decisions.

- **Create timelines to review future presentation opportunities.** This is necessary to ensure presentation standards continue to be a priority. The goal is to move on from presentation basics to deeper issues in the environment. You should schedule frequent meetings initially until you feel the presentation standards are consistent. If the standards are not being met, the meetings should include sales floor walks to evaluate areas, and discuss as a team.

There are many variables to consider with presentation. The team may not be able to order merchandise to fill the shelves or there may be restraints. The team needs to control the things within their parameters. If there are unique circumstances, they should be handled through managers. You cannot accept excuses from your staff for poor presentation. The store presentation can influence customer sales, and it should be considered the basics.

People

The most complex and dynamic area for a broken building is people. Your team, which includes managers and employees, has created the environment that exists today. There are many contributing factors that assist with both good and bad established norms. The previous Store Manager behaviors have contributed to the culture. Their interpretation of the company's vision may have influenced the environment negatively. Your people understand the difference between a manager that cares about people or just the business and they establish norms around the situation.

The goal to repairing a negative environment is to connect and value people. There has to be an open, learning environment for employees to grow in their roles. This cannot be neatly wrapped up in a day, no matter how effective you are at leading people. People have to learn to trust that you mean what you say. Employees will watch your actions closely. For example, you may be passionate about customer service, and preach about the importance of acknowledging customers. If employees and managers watch you on the sales floor pass by customers without speaking to them, it will blow your credibility.

There is no guaranteed recipe for success when it comes to strengthening the culture. There are so many variables that a one-size-fits-all approach is tough to follow. There are several key elements that should be included with any quality plan. The Store Manager needs to be visible and the leader with connecting to people. The following are suggestions to begin healing the culture through developing people.

- **The first step is visibility and connecting to people.** The best way to change the environment is to be visible within it. If you are handed a broken store or if you are trying to figure out the undercurrents of a store, start with walking and talking with employees. This allows you to gain insight into the established norms that exist. It is a great way to blend business and personal conversations to connect with people. You need to learn where the opportunities exist and rebuild through developing your Assistant and Department Managers. Your managers can then connect and develop employees. This is your opportunity to lead by example. You can straighten shelves as you walk, assist customers and hold general connecting conversations with employees. There are probably a million other things that need to be accomplished, but you cannot be a positive influence on people if you are never on the sales floor.

⊃ **Presence at morning, afternoon, evening huddles.** If your company has these huddles, it is a great opportunity to connect and offer guidance. You can get the same message out to a group of people. You can recognize employees for their accomplishments that align with developing the new environment. This is not the opportunity for coaching or negative interactions. You can discuss opportunity areas in general but never highlight an individual in front of their peers for a negative issue. Discuss the opportunities as a group. For example, your customer service scores were low during the last survey. Talk about the current state and what it will take to get to the desired state. Include individuals in the conversation, it will increase buy-in and commitment. Too often managers like to pontificate their thoughts for hours. Keep the huddles focused, educational and appreciative for the work the team is performing. In addition, the time allotted should be short to get the team back to work.

⊃ **Attend sales team meetings.** If your company requires sales meetings for large ticket sales groups, it is a good idea to attend a portion of the meeting. Assistant Managers typically lead these meetings. You do not need to attend the entire session, rather, pop in and discuss some of the wins and outstanding performances. This is another connecting opportunity. You can address issues as a group, and include the team in making decisions and creating solutions. This will increase the commitment level of the team and buy-in to change.

- **Coach, train and develop managers.** It is necessary to develop your management team. You need to assess the current state of managers. This usually takes place as Store Managers meet with Assistant Managers. This is a one-on-one meeting to discuss expectations. You need to review the most recent performance review and numerical data to assist with finding opportunity areas to develop. You need to know where their skill set needs to be strengthened to enable a focus on that area. You cannot focus on all aspects of management. The goal is to develop the weaker areas to improve their overall performance. There is a balance that must exist between development and accountability. A manager will grow through both elements. As we have discussed, there is a double duty that exists with development. The Assistant Manager must continue to work on their developmental areas while coaching their managers and employees to develop in their role. The Store Manager has to teach them to accomplish both at the same time. Keep in mind that managers establish both good and bad norms the same as employees. You cannot demand that a manager understand the business in a different way, You have to teach them.

- **Ensure employee development to strengthen the culture.** A Store Manager cannot personally train everyone in the building.

You need to rely on your management staff to ensure employees receive training. The training is needed to grow in their roles. Your role is to validate that the environment is conducive to learning. The best way to support your management team's effort to develop employees is through recognition. Keep in mind, the right environment for development consists of employees that have clearly defined roles and expectations. You should have open, and honest communication with employees to ensure barriers are being reduced for personal and professional success. You should continually challenge managers to improve with connecting to people and developing the workforce.

- **Ensure all training is completed.** This is a key element to the ongoing learning of your team. Most large retailers have computer based learning programs designed to refresh an employee or managers knowledge base. While these programs will never take the place of mentoring, they contribute to an employee's continuous desire to grow in their position. This is usually an HR function, which may require validation. You should put one of your Assistant Managers in charge of validating training courses. This puts another set of eyes on the process, but also highlights the importance of educating the team. Your role is to ensure the Assistant is taking it seriously and placing a priority on learning.

- **Inspire a coaching environment.** A coaching environment is a collaborative environment. You need to be approachable with a consistent practice of connecting with people. Your team will watch and learn from your examples, both good and bad. An inspirational Store Manager cares about the people that comprise the team. They care through balancing an employee's developmental needs with accountability. They inspire through taking customer service and success seriously. They also help to remove barriers and celebrate the wins with the team. Learn to value and appreciate the team that drives results for your store.

- **Anticipate employee resistance to change.** During the initial transition from a familiar Store Manager to a new one, employees will react in different ways. You can expect there to be some level of resistance. People become uneasy during change. They do not know how their established norms will be interrupted. Even if they see you moving in the right direction, they will be cautious in trusting your leadership. Employee resistance is a cry for communication. Throughout your initial impressions and stages of change, there is a need to communicate the good and the bad. The more you communicate, the more the team will begin to trust you. If your communications include lies or downplays pending change, your team will never trust managers. The relationship between employees and managers is delicate. You need to be up front and communicate change. You need to use communication in the right context. As we have discussed, your communication should be time and place sensitive. If there are changes that will be perceived as negative, you may not want to communicate them during a huddle. You should expect resistance and counter with communication.

People will be the most time consuming element in the broken building. Employees are also the most valuable resource in a broken building. You need to take time to evaluate the capabilities of the staff before you start making changes. Your predecessor may not have placed value on developing people, and the culture along with the morale tanked. This does not automatically mean that all of the people are bad and need to go. There will be a percentage that need to be replaced, but you cannot act until you understand the environment.

Too often, a manager entering a known broken building wants to clean house and make their mark on the store. They want to give the impression that they are serious, and the business will succeed under their guidance. Making uninformed decisions like this will distance the team from your leadership. It will be counterproductive. Your people want the dead weight gone as well, but they need to see that informed decisions are being made. Invest time in the environment of your people to ensure your greatest resource knows they are the greatest resource.

Processes

Broken processes are a part of a damaged environment. Damaged environments produce poor morale and unproductive behavior. The team will find ways around completing processes. When processes are avoided or completed half way, people begin to establish norms to fit the process. Employees may skip elements of processes or make their own rules fit the assignment based on what is important to them.

It is impossible to master every process in a large store. Store Managers need to depend on their management staff to understand processes that impact their areas. Many retailers have an Administrative Manager that is involved with replenishment and operational processes. Your team needs to know where to find information related to processes. If managers are questioning a non-selling function such as receiving or replenishment, they should know where to gain clarification. This also goes for presentation standards or employee policies.

Your organization may have a check sheet or guide for processes. If there are printed materials to simplify or clarify processes, insist your team use them. This information would offer a direction for the team to ensure the processes are complete. Your role, Store Manager, is validation through spot checking the processes. You can organize your efforts to validate essential processes. The following are suggestions to ensure nothing slips through the cracks.

- **Create a daily/ weekly/ monthly checklist.** Too often, processes fail because they are overlooked or forgotten. There are processes that need to be completed at different time periods.

You need to get your team organized, and raise the level of awareness for completing a process. If your organization has a guide or check sheet, train your staff to use it daily. Keep the check sheet in a central location for validation.

If your organization does not have a guide to use, create one. During one of your regularly scheduled meetings, discuss the importance of process completion and your expectations going forward. Assistant Managers should create a checklist with processes that need to be completed every day, week and month. If there are processes that need to be signed-off or tasks that are critical to the daily business, they should be included.

The checklist should be simple and easy to follow. There should be daily, weekly and monthly columns that list the process to be completed. The checklist should have an area, next to the process, for the days of the week. There needs to be an area for initials, as well. The goal is for the opening manager to begin validating processes with afternoon and evening managers assisting throughout the day. This will ensure processes are being completed. It also assigns accountability to your staff.

Consider a brief meeting, 15 minutes or less, in the late afternoon. This is an opportunity to meet with your Assistant Managers. The meeting should center around a discussion of what has been completed and still needs to be done. Store Managers should have a clipboard on their office wall, within eyesight. This will validate that managers are signing off on the processes. Store Managers can see that processes are being monitored, and they can hold a manager accountable if they are not following the sheet. This simple sheet will help to identify breakdowns in completing processes. You will also see significant improvement and a higher rate of completion.

The meeting will add emphasis to following company processes. It will provide a brief update and get everyone on the same page. Do not let the meeting go beyond fifteen minutes; it will become unproductive. The meeting should be held daily regardless if the Store Manager is off for the day. The team can meet quickly to ensure the issues between the day and night shifts are assigned.

⮕ **Ensure your team knows how to find policies.** Large-scale retailers have hundreds of policies. It is tough to know and understand each one of the policies. Your team needs to know where to find policy information to base decisions. You need to encourage them to look at policies before making decisions that require clarity. This helps the staff learn where to find the policies and encourages them to make balanced decisions.

Part of developing your managers is teaching them to make more informed decisions. Your managers should be able to present a change concept that is complete with research of policies and procedures. They may find their view is in opposition to the company's vision or policies prohibit it. This will ensure ideas are well thought out and align with policies.

Once a Store Manager has people, presentation and processes underway they can begin to look at other areas that need addressed. A Retail Consultant would look at these larger issues to begin rebuilding the environment. It is difficult to get to the details with morale in bad shape. If you do not focus on people first, other initiatives will fail. You need the buy-in and commitment to change from employees and managers for successful implementation of initiatives.

You are the consultant in your store. You have the ability to assess the store and identify opportunities. A consultant would tell a manager that rebuilding morale is the key to repairing the store. Regardless of the plan, the Store Manager has to lead the charge for change. You need to connect with people and provide open, honest communication. You must lead by example for change in a broken building. Planning is only effective if you believe in it. Organize your efforts, develop your managers and be accessible to employees on a consistent basis. Change in a broken building is a slow, trusting process that requires visible leadership.

CHAPTER 8

CUSTOMER ENGAGEMENT

Retail Consultants focus on customer engagement from a high level. They work with leaders in your organization to create plans to increase the level of satisfaction customers receive. Store Managers will not typically see consultants in a single unit. Consultants work with your corporate office to create policies and best practices. The corporate leaders in your organization determine your customer engagement practices. They make decisions in regards to frequency and length of interaction. There are various policies on customer engagement depending on the retailer.

Customer service policies created solely at a corporate headquarters runs the risk of being out of touch with what happens in the field. If manager and employee feedback is included with decision making, it helps to bring what customers want into focus.

Corporations need to create a unified approach to servicing customers to ensure they have the best shot at completing a sale. They create service standards to capture as much of the business as possible.

Customer engagement is creating a relationship with the customer to generate a sale today and future visits. Engagement has different meanings for companies. A consumer will require much more assistance planning a kitchen cabinet project in a home improvement retailer than buying a toaster in a discount retailer. There is not one universal approach. Some retailers do not offer assistance unless asked because they feel it represents the customer expectation in their store. Customers have different expectations based upon their perceived level of need in the shopping environment.

Customer Power

There has been a shift a power from retailers to consumers with the advent of the Internet and the recent recession. The recession brought a cautious spending outlook and customers changed the strategy for many retailers. Customers abandoned the mid price point selections and demanded quality at a lower price. Retailers began focusing on value price points to keep business alive through tight consumer spending. Payroll was reduced in favor of lower margin sales and customers understood the trade-off.

During this transition, consumers began to realize the power of choice and various ways to buy. Customers emerged from the slow, ongoing recovery with more knowledge and expectations of retailers. The demand in retail today is customer service, selection, price and a web presence.

Technology has influenced buying decisions for customers. No longer does a customer need to travel to several different retailers for price or selection. They can scroll through a competitor's inventory on their phone while they are in your store. This makes customer engagement even more crucial because stores may only have a small window to make an impression and get the sale.

Customers have become more demanding, but basic service principles still apply. Customers can be kept in your store or encouraged to return depending on their store experience. It is imperative that your team understands the value of their interaction with customers. Your team needs to provide the right service or beyond the expected level of service. The customer may decide to stay in the store and buy.

Customer Feedback

One of the best places to start to understand your customers is directly from your customers. A Retail Consultant that wants to know what the customer thinks of the store would go right to the source. They would design questionnaires that ask the customer their thoughts on the entire shopping experience. Store Managers may not be able to issue a questionnaire depending on the company's policy, but you do not need it to get customer feedback.

This does not require a formal survey. Most of the great customer service Store Managers are known for bringing their enthusiasm to the sales floor. They do not fear talking to customers and have no problem interacting with them in the aisles. Your company may require Store Managers to be on the sales floor for a specific number of hours or part of your day. Regardless, use your time on the floor to learn and value customers. The following are a few suggestions for Store Managers on the sales floor.

- **Speak to every customer encountered.** This is for two reasons. First, you are leading by example for employees. Second, it gives you the opportunity to ask customers about their experience. This could be a simple question such as *"Are we helping with everything you need today?"* You may be surprised at the answer.

- **Walk and talk with customers.** There is probably a good portion of your time walking customers to an area of the store. You should not point or give directions, rather, walk the customer to what they are seeking. While you are walking, ask the customer how often they are in the store. Ask about what they like or what frustrates them. This information is valuable, and it does not require a list of questions. Let your interaction be natural and not forced.

⊃ **Appreciate your customers, often.** While you are on the sales floor, it is a great opportunity to thank the customer for choosing your store. Consider your last shopping experience in a retailer. Did a manager acknowledge your presence in the store? This is the point. It does not happen. You should value your customer's decision to be in the store, there are plenty of options. If you appreciate the customers, your employees will value them, as well.

The feedback should be shared with your team, both positive and negative. You need to encourage your management team to solicit feedback from customers. They should ask for immediate feedback when a customer has a complaint about service. The wins should be shared during huddle and staff meetings. The gauge of service success in your store will come from one source, your customers. The customer decides if your service is as good as you think it is. Your job is to continually adjust and react to the feedback.

Store Managers need to give their Assistant Managers quotas at first to gather feedback. The goal is for customer conversations to become part of their established norms. You need to discuss the value customer feedback represents to the store. Helping customers should be the expectation. Connecting with customers also helps to identify stock issues, competitive advantages and current trends.

Department Managers/ Employee Inclusion Groups

The closest group to the customer in a retail store is the Department Managers and employees. They are on the front lines and interact with the customer on a daily basis. Since they have their finger on the pulse of sales and trends, it makes sense to value their input. The problem with most retailers is they really do not seek input from Department Managers or employees. Typically, Store and Assistant Managers are making a majority of the decisions when it comes to inventory and customer service. Leaving out the front line team is neglecting a huge piece to the customer service puzzle.

There are two suggestions to tap into the closest resource your store has to the customer. First, collaborate with Department Managers to learn about customer expectations. Second, organize an employee inclusion group that heightens awareness of both the good and bad that exists in the shopping environment. Both of these suggestions can be used simultaneously, or you can utilize one. Any program that you create to bring the voice of the customer to the store is beneficial.

- **Department Manager collaboration.** This can be a formal or informal approach, but it should be structured to offer guidance. Larger retailers have several meetings that take place weekly. If your store has a meeting that includes Department Managers, it is a great opportunity to tap into their knowledge. If your current meeting structure does not include Department Managers, consider an invitation to them for a specific time during the session. They should come prepared to briefly discuss customer feedback for the week. They should identify barriers to success and possible solutions. This accomplishes two things. First, it brings managers closer to customer needs and concerns. Second, it develops your managers to recognize barriers and create solutions. Your role is to guide them through the solution process and help them see their solution connected to the whole system. If managers collaborate with their department, they will learn and teach at the same time. Your team will learn how to identify problems and create long-term solutions.

- **Organize an employee inclusion group.** The beauty of this approach is empowering employees to create solutions for customer concerns. This approach also brings the voice of the customer to managers and highlights the success and opportunities within the store. Store Managers do not have enough time in a week to listen to all of the feedback that employees possess. Managers need to have an organized way to hear employees and customers. One suggestion is creating an employee inclusion team. This will accomplish two things. First, you will hear the concerns of your team for customers and the environment. Second, you should assign the team to an Assistant Manager to assist with their development. The following are suggestions for the inclusion team.

- **The inclusion team should be comprised of diverse employees from various areas of the store.** Be sure to include non-selling, administrative areas, as well. You want as many different perspectives to offer a complete view of the environment. The group should number approximately 10 members.

- **The team should meet once per month for 1 hour.** The meeting should be administered by an Assistant or HR Manager. Their role is to keep the meeting moving and take notes. The manager should not interrupt the conversation or use the time for other issues. They should assist with developing solutions to problems.

- **The team should have an agenda to follow to keep the meeting on topic.** The goal of the meeting is to learn about barriers for employees and customers. The team should be free to speak, in a respectful manner; about issues they feel hinder sales and service. An agenda will help support a productive meeting and reduce complaints that do not produce solutions.

- **The Assistant Manager should lead the discussion for solutions to the problems.** This is an opportunity for the manager to guide the team and connect the proposed solution to the whole system. This will reduce time invested in unrealistic solutions or creating solutions that violate policies.

- **The Assistant Manager and Store Manager should meet to discuss the issues and solutions generated from the meeting.** Your role is to offer guidance to the Assistance Manager and support initiatives that can improve the environment.

Your organization may have a structure in place for feedback from employees and managers. The best advice is to use the program and use it consistently. It will send the message to your team that managers care about their issues and value their input. If your company has no established programs, then consider the options discussed. The options will not take much time away from other things but will support a learning environment and customer connection.

Quotes

Your organization may perform quotes for a customer. Most home improvement stores sell large projects and complete quotes on a daily basis. If employees are handing a customer a quote without understanding their motivations for buying or not buying, they are leaving the quote out there for competitors. Consider a quote an invitation for every other retailer to take the sale from your store. The employee has done all of the hard work qualifying the customer and determining their needs. They hand over the quote with te belief that the customer will not buy anywhere else.

The truth is, quotes are typically shopped around for better pricing. Customers will take the hard work and time investment from your employees and get a competitive price in another store. Employees need to be coached, trained and developed to close sales. It is a part of customer engagement in your store. What message does the customer take away with a quote? Does the customer really believe the employee has their best interests in mind?

When an employee hands a customer a price quote, they need to engage the customer in other ways. They need the customer to understand why they should buy from them. Too often, the employee hands the customer information and asks the customer to let them know. This is not customer engagement. The employee needs to make an impression on the customer to buy.

Customer engagement requires making a connection with the customer. It needs to go beyond pricing. Most retailers will meet and beat prices from competitors. The price matching practices are typically highlighted in the store. Customers are aware of the ability of a company to beat the pricing of another retailer. The efforts of your employees should include:

- **Understand the customer's motivators to buy.** The employee should determine time frames, and why the customer wants to buy.

- **Understand the barriers to customer buying.** What factors will keep the customer from buying. Is it price, credit, product assortment? The employee needs to understand the reason to enable them to overcome it.

- **Give the customer a reason to return.** The employee should acknowledge that many customers get other quotes, but ask the customer to give their store the last chance before they buy. The employee is asking for an opportunity to beat competitors.

- **Follow up with the customer.** There are many examples of employees that give a quote and never follow up with the customer to close the sale. The employee needs to follow up to address barriers to customer buying.

Quotes require a further step at connecting with the customer. You should not take it for granted that a customer will naturally return to the store because they have a quote. You need to assume the customer will seek other opinions or prices. The customer dynamic from a sale today to a potential future sale changes dramatically. Your team needs to understand that engagement changes from an immediate decision to a project relationship.

Consultants and Customer Service

A Retail Consultant will often look at customer service levels as a result of policies established by the company. They look for obvious breakdowns in the execution of policies. For example, if your company has a rule that employees acknowledge every customer within a ten foot radius and your team is not consistent with this practice, is it the rule that had failed or execution. Maybe the rule is not effective or does not give enough to customers. This is why it is so valuable to get feedback directly from your customer. Where does the failure exist?

Consultants look at the service piece for ways to increase customer engagement. The main ingredient is attentive employees that begin the conversation. The approach can fall prey to established norms by ignoring company standards in customer service. If your policy states that every customer that an employee or manager comes in contact with should be greeted, and they are allowed to walk by the customer, there is approval of the behavior. If managers are not going to correct policy violations, they are part of the problem.

Managers that violate policies are also guilty of endorsing bad norms. You need to review the customer service policies for your company. After the review, you need to observe the interaction between customers and managers or employees. If your team is not adhering to the policies, it needs to be addressed. You need to discuss the value of customer interaction to the store.

Your team may be adhering to the policies, but there may be an opportunity to enhance the level of service. You need to collaborate with the team to determine additional measures. The collaboration helps to strengthen commitment to change and promotes buy-in. A consideration should be your direct competitor. How does your competitor acknowledge customers and encourage engagement? Your competitor may be less effective than your store. This does not mean your store is doing everything it can to promote engagement. The goal is to be the best. Being just a little better than competitors is not enough.

There is a noticeable difference between customer centric stores and less focused units. In a customer centric environment, employees acknowledge your existence and are available for help. In other stores, employees and managers will walk right by customers and look the other way. They have names for customers like "guests", but they do not live up to their own perception of customer service. These retailers may equally be successful. Which type of store truly engages the customer?

Every employee should acknowledge a customer that is encountered. This does not mean that they have to stop their work in progress. They need to say hello, which at least lets the customer know they have some value to the retailer. Some of the most effective Store Managers are dynamic in front of customers. They have personalities and interact with customers on the sales floor. A Retail Consultant would look at your engagement level with customers as well as the team. Would they find a Store Manager that leads by example or one that is part of the norm?

A Retail Consultant would determine the level of customer engagement through observation. You should not just utilize reporting or customer surveys to determine your level of success with customers. Keep in mind, even successful stores that are performing well may have opportunities with customer engagement. You need to observe the interactions of your team while you are on the sales floor. Here are a few questions to keep in mind while observing customer engagement.

- **Are employees approaching customers or do customers need to ask for help?**
- **Are there any examples of customers that have not been acknowledged while employees perform task work?**
- **Are there examples of employees or managers walking by customers without acknowledging them?**
- **Do neighboring departments help customers when there is high traffic in an area?**
- **How many customers are noticed in aisles without assistance?**
- **Are there examples of outstanding customer service and how is the department performing for the year? Is there a**

correlation between departments that provide service and their performance?
- Are there customer wins that can be noted and shared with the group during a huddle?
- Walking your floor in the eyes of a customer, what type of environment is noticed?

What does your sales floor feel like when walking throughout the store? Is the environment open and welcoming or does it feel closed and chaotic? There is a definite "feel" to a store environment. The more experience you accumulate, the more in touch you become with retail environments.

There are several ways to encourage an engaged culture. Most include enforcing new standards that focus on the customer. You need to work within the company guidelines, and not create initiatives that are in direct opposition to policies. The following are suggestions to develop a customer centric environment.

- **Lead by example and speak to every customer encountered.**
- **Ensure to communicate expectations at meetings and huddles. Every manager and employee acknowledges every customer, no exceptions.**
- **Schedule tasks around peak traffic times.**
- **Enforce customer service expectations by following company disciplinary policies for managers and employees that do not follow the program.**

- **Recognize employees and managers for great examples of customer service. Celebrate great customer interactions at huddles and meetings.**
- **Discuss the present state and desired state of customer service standards at huddles and meetings.**
- **Assign Assistant Managers to complete customer surveys.**
- **Assemble employee inclusion teams to identify barriers and create solutions.**

All of the suggestions require consistent validation and enforcement by you. If you do not validate the programs that you want the team to utilize, it will appear that you do not care about it. The team will develop norms in response to your lack of involvement in a program. They will essentially work around the Store Manager. It needs to be a priority for you to be a priority for Assistant Managers. You need to challenge your team to continually improve the service level they offer customers.

CHAPTER 9

COMPETITIVE DIAGNOSIS

An area that a Retail Consultant would examine is the state of competition. Store Managers cannot ignore the influence competitors have over their business. The competition is part of the whole system. You need to consider competitors when you are creating plans for change or solving problems. The competition represents a powerful force for taking wallet share from customers.

Diagnosing the components of a competitor is not an easy task. There is a lot of information available online for publically traded companies. You can review financial performance of a competitor through the investor portion of their website. The annual statement will typically discuss the success of the previous year and opportunities. The statement will also provide an outlook for the upcoming year. This information is good from a high level but does not provide nearly enough data for your local market. To gain insight into local efforts, you need to understand how the local store operates.

Analyze the Environment

Competitors have the same problems in their environment as your store. They face the same pressures to succeed and retain talent. The Store Managers are trying to leverage their strengths and create a solution to drive more business. They may be in your building, talking with your sales people and reviewing your presentation standards. The goal is to gain insight into what makes your building a preference to consumers. The reason competitors want to know is to strengthen areas where they have a competitive advantage. They also want to adjust areas where they are currently at a disadvantage.

There are many variables in the equation of competitors in your building. The managers may not do a thorough job at understanding your environment. They may perform a few price comparisons assuming that price is the only thing that matters. If they identify areas that give their store the competitive advantage, they may not know how to disseminate the information to their teams. There are two things to consider with competitive intelligence.

➲ **What competitive information is necessary to learn?**

➲ **What does your team do with the information?**

The competitor may be awful at handling this information. They are probably in your store but may do a horrible job at gaining any insight or utilizing the information they gather. The main reason competitive intelligence is rarely realized is the thought process behind understanding a competitor. The main drive for most managers is solely pricing. They view the competition by the price that will win the customer. They neglect the other attributes of a store that may represent value to a customer.

If there is an opportunity for your competitor to improve with their evaluation of your business, there is a strong probability that there is an opportunity for your store to improve your assessment. If you approach a competitive analysis with a pricing focus, you are missing many other elements that comprise the customer experience. Price is an important issue, but it is not the only consideration for customers when choosing a place to buy. Customers like to buy from retailers, where they find a level of trust and comfort. They want a retailer to deliver value and selection in a pleasant environment.

When walking through the doors of a competitor, what should a Store Manager hope to learn? If you are going to just check out any changes or promotional efforts, you are not maximizing the visit. The goal of the visit should be planned. You need to learn the inner workings of the store. You need to look at the store through the eyes of a customer. Here are a few questions you should answer when analyzing a competitor.

- What can be learned about the environment?
- What can be learned about the people and established norms?
- What can be learned about customer service standards?
- Is there consistency with the presentation standards?
- What is your advantage over this competitor?
- What are your disadvantages with this competitor?
- Why do customers want to buy from this competitor?
- Why would customers want to shop there instead of your store?

You need to analyze the competitor beyond the surface. The same as your store has undercurrents; the competitor has them, as well. You want to analyze the whole system that makes up the environment. Clearly, you will not have the reporting or natural insight into the competitor's environment. You have the opportunity to experience the competitor as a customer. This requires time in the store and an agenda. You need to take the questions and figure out what you want to learn from the store.

Competitor Shops

The best way to discover what the competition has to offer is through scheduled competitive shops. A Retail Consultant would investigate what a Store Manager knows about competitors and how the team gathers and disseminates information. You need to look at your current practices. You also need to review company policies to determine your effectiveness. If your company has a competitive shop program in place, your team should be using it. You cannot be the only one inside of a competitor's store. Your team needs to be involved, as well.

If your company does not have a formal program, it is imperative that one is created. You need to consider the competition as a part of the whole system. Competitors influence your store and wallet share with customers. You need to take them seriously. You need to have your finger on the pulse of competitors to be proactive and reactive to market needs. The following suggestions are to get your competitive program in motion.

- **Create a list of competitors in your market.** The depth of the list depends on your store surroundings. Heavily populated retail areas will require an effort to prioritize competitive influences. You should prioritize the competitors by direct and indirect threats. Your direct competitors are those that are most like your business. They have similar inventories and cater to the same type of customer. The other retailers should be considered by the majority of lines matched to additional retailers that may only carry a few of the lines as your store. The purpose of prioritizing is to establish a routine for visits. You want to continually be inside of the competitors that take the most market share.

⮕ **Create a plan for visiting competitors.** There are two items to consider with planning competitive visits. First, who will complete the competitor store visits. There are absolutes that must be scheduled to complete visits. The Store, Assistant, and Department Managers must be part of the regular rotation to perform visits. This allows them to gain insight in to competitive environments. You may also want key sales people involved, as well. This is typically high-volume sales positions. Second, you need to consider the frequency of visits. The goal is to be inside of high-priority retailers every 30 days. This will allow your team to understand the environment and notice subtle changes. This should be scheduled at different times throughout a month. This will allow coverage throughout the month to capture small changes and notice various implementations. The smaller retailers can be spread out to every other month or a time-period that you feel appropriate to understand the environment.

⮕ **Prepare initial research of competitors.** Your team should prepare for the upcoming visits. The focus should be narrowed to one or two objectives. You need to have a narrowed, structured focus to actually learn from the visit. If you go with no focus, you will waste time walking around looking for something that differentiates the competitor from your store. You can stagger the visits to keep the team regularly updated on the competitor. You should consider the following four questions in your visit preparation:

1. **What specific products, programs or customer service initiatives does the team need to gain further insight about the competitor?**
2. **What can be learned about the competitor's environment?**
3. **What specific information needs to return to the store from the visit?**
4. **Why would a customer choose this competitor?**

- **Managers should focus on their areas to be competitive experts.** Your managers and sales people completing the visits should stick to their area of expertise. This enables the team to be experts that can share the information with their teams. This allows the individual to understand how the competitor is influencing sales in their area through product, pricing, programs and customer service. If they visit with a broad scope of the competitor, it will result in a generalized review of the environment. You want the individual to recognize changes in the environment and enable them to learn about competitive environments beyond pricing.

A formalized program ensures everyone is working toward the

same goal. It also ensures that visits are productive. Too often, a manager will insist an employee shops the competition and report their findings. The employee will walk around the store looking for promotions and pricing, and everyone considers the visit a success. They need to visit with an objective and learn how the competitor serves the customer. They can then create solutions to service the customer in a more competitive way. They should determine their objectives before they reach the competitor. This will ensure a learning experience that can be shared with the entire team.

Competitive Intelligence

After the information is gathered, how will it reach the individuals that need to utilize it? Gathering the information is half of the battle, the other half is putting the information in motion. The information should be used to close sales and build customer relationships. It should also be used to keep potential customers in the store and keep them from buying at the competition. Your team will have the necessary information to be the destination for the customer.

An Assistant Manager that organizes and distributes the information should administer the competitive program. This furthers their development and emphasizes the importance of competitive intelligence. The information must be disseminated weekly to ensure it reaches employees in time to react. You need to determine the most efficient method of reaching employees with the information.

You may want to consider a weekly email update that gathers all of the competitive intelligence for the week. It does not need to be complicated, or labor intensive, the goal is to get the information to employees regularly. The Assistant Manager should gather information from the scheduled shops and organize the information by area. The note should also state what the employee should do to keep the customer in the store. If email is not available to everyone, consider a printed copy placed in a communication binder at each of the area desks. The Department Manager can review with employees, and they should sign off on the information.

The communication should be printed and hung on a clipboard in the Store and Assistant Manager offices. This ensures a competitive focus is always in view for managers. The competition is a serious component to the whole system. It has to be relevant to the Store Manager for it to be important to the staff. Your job is to validate the process is being completed. You need to report your findings from shops. You will have more insight into the overall environment. To combat the influence of competitors, you need the entire team fighting for sales.

Diagnose the Environment

The people that comprise the competitive environment are the most difficult element to further your knowledge. It is easy to identify changes in presentation or pricing but noticing a change or development in people is more challenging. The only way to gain insight into the culture is by asking the employees for help and gauging their skill level. You need to be alert for their level of professionalism and desire to assist customers. They may not have all of the answers but may overcome their limitations through personality or a connection.

You need to be aware of the top sales people with the competitor. You may need to recruit individuals for jobs. You need to understand the abilities of the best employees inside of the competition. This gives you an opportunity to interact with competitive employees to gauge their selling ability. This does not mean that you walk around and hand your business card to everyone, rather, observe and interact to understand the environment. Here are a few questions to consider when diagnosing the competitors culture.

- When first entering the store, what is the first impression of the environment?
- Do the employees acknowledge your existence in the store?
- Are the employees trained on the product they are selling?

- What are the attitudes of the employees that offered assistance?
- Are there managers present on the sales floor? Did they acknowledge your presence?
- Are there groups of employees talking together away from customers?
- Are employees engaged in task work and not acknowledging customers? What is the demeanor of the customers in the store? Do they seem satisfied?

Think about these questions and your own store. If the competitor was walking through your store, what would they see? You may notice some of the same issue prevalent in the environment. The environment in your competitors building may be in better or worse shape than your store. Though the issues may not tell the whole story on that visit, you can validate your findings on future visits. If the competitor is offering sub-par service, how can your store leverage their weakness into a strength. If your store has issues, how can you change the culture?

It will naturally take more than one visit to a competitor to understand pieces of their environment. It is a complex dynamic and you have limited resources to evaluate the culture. The more that you understand a major competitor, the more you realize the advantages and disadvantages. You cannot assume your store is executing at a higher level than the competition. You need to enter the building without assumptions and bias to analyze the environment.

Control

The Store Manager has local control in competing with other retailers. You have very little control over major corporate decisions. You cannot control location, marketing or policies and procedures. You need to consider these elements when analyzing your competitors, as well as your own store. Even elements you cannot control may influence the business positively or negatively.

Marketing can influence a customer's decision to buy. You may have a sales decline in a product line and may have reviewed the presentation, pricing, inventory and store environment. The elements you have reviewed may show your store and the competitor as comparable. You need to consider the promotional efforts of the competitor. They may have been aggressive in print, television or other avenues of media. You can start focusing on the area with ongoing research of the competitor's efforts.

Advertising products is typically scheduled months in advance of the actual promotion date. This enables buyers to secure product quantities. Store Managers have very little control at the store level with the decisions of marketing and buyers. You may have control in your store over the use of end caps or promotional bulk stacks. If you follow the promotional efforts of the competitor, you may be able to determine the price point or items they spotlight. This will help determine the items to increase inventory and plan additional visibility through end caps or promotional areas.

If there is something that exists in the competitor's environment that gives them an advantage, You need to determine if you can counteract it. There may be policies that exclude you from directly competing. If there are changes that can be made such as inventory, pricing or promotional efforts, you need to track the change and ensure you are getting a return on your investment. You cannot assume that simply placing an item in a more visible spot may increase sales. You need to evaluate the risk, and if it is not paying off, do not wait for results. Promotional places in the store are valuable real estate. You need to protect the space to get the most out of it.

Crush the Competition

Being the best in your market cannot just be a war cry. Your team cannot repeat company cheers at morning huddles and walk away feeling the competition does not matter. The only way to crush the competition is to understand the competition. It is more of a chess match than a boxing match. It involves an intelligent strategy and approach along with consistency to be the better business.

Retail Consultants will look at the competitive culture that managers have created in the store. The Store Manager cannot be the only one in the store with a passion for sales. This is either present in your store culture, or it is lacking. The following are questions to answer in relation to the level of competitive passion in your store:

- **Is there a plan for the team to be inside of major competitors every month? Are the competitive visits productive?**
- **Do you utilize the information learned from competitive shops?**
- **Do managers include the influence of competitors in their planning?**
- **Do sales people have the skills to close sales?**
- **Do your sales people follow up with customers to close sales?**
- **Do your sales people acknowledge customers and have a genuine interest in selling to customers?**
- **Do managers and employees react to customer needs?**
- **Do managers help to remove competitive barriers for the team?**

Crushing the competition is more than a feeling that your store is doing well. You need to be confident that your team takes the competition seriously, and the competitive strategy is working. Like any other plan, you should review the effectiveness and adjust where necessary. Beating the competition takes brains and not bravado. You need to beat competitors through sales, and that takes time and energy. It also takes a cultural change to create a passion for being the best option for customers.

CHAPTER 10

PLANNING FOR SUCCESS

The desire to adopt retail-consulting techniques is both a personal and professional venture. It is a desire to improve your work environment and work on personal development, as well. The more you apply the techniques and a consultative approach, the more they will integrate into your skill-set. You will begin to look at situations, even small issues, in terms of a complete resolution.

Integrating consulting practices into your development plan allows a view of your store through a business lens. It provides a manager tools to enhance their ability to recognize and remove barriers. A consultant mentality gives you a view of the undercurrents that are driving visible results. Thinking and acting like a Retail Consultant is a disciplined approach that expands your natural ability to solve problems and consider the whole system.

What makes a Store Manager a good or bad candidate to think like a consultant? You must be open to evolving in your role. You have to be willing to evaluate your abilities, and the capabilities of your people. You have to be receptive to self-criticism of your skills and ability to lead. These traits and characteristics align Store Managers and Retail Consultants.

Planning vs. Passion for Success

A passion for success is different from a passion for sales. Achieving success is creating a balance in the experience of both customers and employees. Customers need an environment that promotes service, selection and pricing. Employees need an environment that encourages development and accountability. A passion for sales only focuses on one component of the environment. Your sales people should possess a drive for sales and customer service. They are focusing on a singular element of the environment.

There is a point where both environments merge. It merges when a customer meets the people, processes and presentation in your store. The environment for employees will influence customer buying both positively and negatively. If you have established a closed environment, it will show in the results. The results are a recap of customer buying in your store. There are other elements to consider such as inventory, trends and advertising, but it may be the culture in your store for better or worse.

Passion can sometimes overshadow smart decision-making. Store Managers may be driven to win at all costs which influences the way they look at employees and customers. It is a much better policy to change your passion for success to planning for success. Passion is an emotion. While it is good to be excited by wins and your store performance, it is better planning progress and development to succeed.

When you encounter a set-back or disappointment, analyze the problem and adjust your strategy. Having passion to overcome obstacles does not necessarily mean there is a plan. This may mean that you gather your management staff in a room and scream until they are clear that they must fix the problem. This is not a plan. It does not provide direction or help the staff understand the size or scope of the problem. Instead, your managers hit the sales floor and relay the message to employees to shape up or ship out. The only change is disgruntled employees are now assisting customers.

A better approach is getting the managers in the room and discussing how to correct the situation. Talk about barriers and what practices or training can be implemented to change the culture or established norms. It may require a drastic change for employees. Your role is to bridge the gap between the current state and the desired state. If you want to express emotion, show the team what the future state looks like after the problem is fixed.

Not all planning has a positive path to the desired state. There may be extreme measures required to handle a problem. The good news with planning is your staff can see the finish line. You can see where the changes will lead. It is a proactive approach to resolving a situation. Too often, a passion for success is reactive and has no structure to get to a goal. The goal in most cases is undefined, other than reversing a problem.

Consultants plan for success. They are disciplined to create plans for execution. Every plan must have checkpoints to ensure it is still on target. They get passionate about buy-in and willingness to change. Consultants get excited over collaboration and contributions to planning. They deliver the message with a conviction to develop a long-term solution. They want their client to win as much as managers want their store to win. Ultimately, both roles want the same thing.

The Store Manager Advantage

There are many advantages a Store Manager has in their store. You can see progress and the success or failure of implementations. You have a better understanding of what motivates your employees across the store. You already have insight into your market and some of the influences on the business. The Store

Manager is an Internal Consultant. They need to practice the disciplines to claim this role.

Along with the Internal Consultant designation comes the insight and baggage of that role. You gain the crucial element of time by already knowing the policies and expectations of the company. You understand the current performance level of the store. You also have insight into established norms and the potential of managers and employees.

The baggage or downside a Store Manager brings to the Internal Consultant role is their bias. Managers may believe their leadership is better than it really is which may influence their decision-making. You have an attachment to people, which may cloud your business judgment and cause you to overlook performance issues. It may also be challenging to adopt the disciplines and practices into your routine. It requires patience, practice and hard work.

You have a significant advantage by being close to the environment. You have the ability to diagnose, and create solutions much quicker than learning the entire structure. Your opportunity will be learning the nuances that exist within the culture that were never noticed before. A Retail Consultant or External Consultant would require a significant amount of time to understand the environment, its people and activities. You must use your knowledge and experience to your advantage.

New Store Managers

New Store Managers have the task of trying to lead people while trying to figure out their management style. You may be placed in a store with many established norms courtesy of the previous manager. Some norms will be productive while others will be destructive to the environment. You have the unenviable task of sorting them out and learning as you go along. You have inherited the problems and the successes.

Taking on the workload of a new Store Manager and adopting the consulting principles may seem overwhelming. The consulting principles are a great way to begin discovering your environment. It will help in making long-term plans. Teaching the principles to your management staff will develop their skills. It will also help present barriers and solution plans for guidance. You will not need to start at the beginning of the process once your managers are informed, rather, offer advice and possible alternate solutions.

Remember that teaching the consulting principles reinforces your own learning and understanding of practices used by consultants. There is no shortcut or abbreviated way to diagnose your environment. If you are going to plan for success, you need to consider all of the elements as a tenured Store Manager. You may have an advantage. You have not yet established bad habits or influenced the environment. It may be less work for a new manager to integrate practices because there are less negative habits established.

Your Coaching & Accountability Style

Along with changing the way you approach problems and develop the environment, you may find a change in your coaching style. Your style may change naturally as you adapt to new ways of thinking and viewing the business. Your change may also be planned in response to leveraging effective behaviors and eliminating ineffective traits.

Finding a coaching style that works is essential to developing a learning environment. A coach offers guidance. There is a fine line between coaching and control. You cannot coach through utilizing an aggressive approach. You need to find a balance between education, guidance and feedback. You want the team to view you as a resource for learning. Coaching creates an open environment. It is necessary for uniting the team to work towards the vision.

Here are a few considerations for coaching:

- **Coaching is for long-term growth.**
- **Coaching supports continuous employee development.**
- **Coaching should be separate from discipline and goal setting. Recognition should be used to set positive examples for the**

team.
- ➲ **Coaching will improve your culture.**
- ➲ **Coaching will lead to a more productive team.**
- ➲ **Coaching will develop future managers for the company.**

Keep your coaching efforts pure. Do not dilute coaching by increasing or setting goals. You need to continue coaching as a guiding tool to enhance the skills of employees and managers. Part of a Store Managers role is to assess capabilities of their team to build a future bench of promotable employees and managers. Coaching not only offers guidance, but it also increases the interaction between you and the team to help with assessing their abilities.

Accountability is as important as coaching. On one hand, you are giving the team the tools to improve their skills. On the other hand, you have a higher level of expectation. Both are necessary to build a high performance team. You need to manage down the middle of connecting and coaching people with accountability measures. Accountability should not be a scary term for managers. It simply means the manager or employee has a clear understanding of their role and the expectations attached to the position.

Accountability keeps the balance in a retail environment. It ensures the staff is pulling their weight and contributing to the success of the store. Accountability keeps the hierarchy of the store structure in place. It is a gauge for managerial delegation and validation of assignments. Accountability levels the playing field in the store and gives everyone a fair work environment.

Learning Plans

You cannot hope to make changes in the environment, development and managerial abilities at the same time without a plan. You need to have a learning plan. This is nothing more than a personal calendar where you write down what you want to put into action for the week or longer period. This should be separate from your other calendars or agenda. This should be a personal plan that lists learning, teaching and implementation for the week.

The plan could be a part of the consulting principles, or other ideas you want to sample to see if they fit into your management style. This gives managers the chance to really think and feel if they understand the value of the plan. Managers may need to extend their learning or shorten the time allotted. There are no hard and fast rules; it is your personal agenda for development.

Store Managers may want to alternate the plan between learning and teaching. For example, a manager may want to spend a week or two on the diagnosis part of the retail consulting principles. The following week, they may want to teach Assistants about diagnosing problems. They have a chance to understand the material first and then reinforce their learning through teaching others. The immediate week following the teaching sessions, managers may want to schedule a learning exercise. Take a problem in the store and work your way through the principles to create a solution.

The following is an example of what a learning plan may look like in your planner.

Month Goal: Learn/ Teach Step 4 of The Retail Consulting Principles

- Week One: Learn, The Retail Consulting Principles: Step 4 Connecting The Whole System.
- Week Two: Teach two Assistant Managers, The Retail Consulting Principles: Step 4 Connecting The Whole System.
- Week Three: Teaching Exercise, Staffing in Electronics Department/ Connect to the Whole System.
- Week Four: Reflect on Learning and Teaching Whole System Principles.

A learning plan begins with the larger goal stated at that top. What do you want to accomplish in personal growth for the month? The goal is the big picture. The next step is breaking down the goal into individual components each week. The weekly goals are the details for learning required to reach the goal.

The weekly goals will help to organize your approach to learning. They are the roadmap to the end goal. They should be detailed. If you are reviewing printed material or websites, you may want to define resources and schedule them by day. You want the goals to be obtainable considering all other facets of life. If you try to force too much into a week, there is a greater chance of abandoning the learning plan because you feel overwhelmed. Make the plan reasonable, the goal is to learn a new skill, which takes time.

The final week is allotted for reflecting on both the learning and teaching aspects of the month. Reflection is dedicating time to reviewing your actions and considering alternatives. This is especially helpful if there is not success in reaching the goal. You may consider continuing with the topic over the next week or longer. You may need additional time or resources for the teaching aspect of the goal.

Reflection offers clarity in not only the message but how it was received and delivered. You may need additional resources or a different resource to gain insight into a specific topic. You may gather information on the goal from your Assistants. You can invest time in learning to really understand the topic and the application of it in your job.

Reflection time helps to adjust the pace of learning. You may need to add to the calendar to increase the pace or reduce the number of weekly components. You want to develop a plan to enhance your skill set. Another use for reflection is thinking about a past problem and applying new knowledge to it. What would be done differently? How does your new skill allow the problem to be seen in a different way? Ask yourself questions to test your understanding and advance the skill.

Integrity

Retail Consultants and Store Managers need to have integrity for the consulting process. Integrity is a high sense of morals, ethics and honesty in everything you do. These traits are instilled in Store Managers that lead by example and consistent with their actions. Integrity also shows a genuine care for your people and business.

You also have a bond of integrity that exists between you and the boss. The expectation is that you know policies and adhere to company standards for employees and customers. The planning and solutions created are trusted to be within the guidelines of the company. There are instances where taking a short cut or sacrificing ethics will be tempting. The sacrifices never work out well.

The retail consulting principles are rendered useless if they are based on policy violations. You will never create long-term change if you base solutions on dishonesty. You are jeopardizing your career and trust with people. Integrity is also a bond between you and other managers and employees. You expect your people to complete tasks, generate solutions and interact with customers with integrity.

Trust has to be earned through all avenues in life. Trust is rarely given without earning it. You must lead people with integrity. If you violate trust, you may never get it back. You may think you have a better way to do business that opposes company policies and procedures. You must adhere to the structure provided by your corporate office. Once you stray outside of the boundaries, you have lost an important element in business and life, your integrity.

The Journey

The purpose of this book is to show the value of integrating consulting practices into your analysis and decision-making. When you integrate these practices, you make business decisions with your head and not your heart. You need to connect with people and care about them, but you cannot base your decision-making on how you feel about people. You need to base decisions on thorough business analysis and the influence of and on the whole system.

There is not the expectation of becoming a professional consultant. The advantage of a consultant is applying problem solving techniques in varied environments. You develop solutions by reflecting on past successes and creating plans based on principles. You get to see different things in different assignments. You learn to apply your practices to smaller problems and daily situations. As you become more comfortable with analyzing situations and thinking through solutions, you will begin to adapt these practices to daily problems.

Your journey begins as a learning process. The retail consulting principles are your guide to a more complete view of your world. The journey continues as you teach teams the principles to develop their skills. You do not want to be the only one on staff that understands how to strengthen success or create solutions for problems.

Your staff should have the ability to analyze situations, and bring solutions to you for guidance. They are learning to consider all options, and they get the benefit of your wisdom to support or adjust the plan. You get the benefit of solutions presented and not just problems. It saves time and develops your staff. Your managers will be more committed to a plan that they helped to create. It will promote buy-in, and they will work to see the plan succeed.

You can identify and repair problems in your environment, but only if you understand what is causing the issue. You need a solid understanding of how the problem influences other parts of the system. You cannot continue to apply surface logic and rushed solutions to problems. This type of problem solving only leads to a wider distribution of the problem and additional issues for employees and customers.

Let's not forget why you became a Store Manager. You want to increase sales and profits through creating an exciting and helpful experience for your customers. You want to teach and develop your team to be better at what they do and create a bench of future leaders. Your team wants success and potential opportunities to advance their career. Personal development is essential to continuing growth in your role. You can be the Retail Consultant in your store through determination and personal planning.

ABOUT THE AUTHOR

Richard Bell has been in retail management for the past 23 years. He has held various leadership positions in small and big-box retailers. He published the book Coaching, Training & Developing The Retail Manager in 2012 and The Retail Leadership Bridge in 2013. He has a Master of Science in Management degree with a specialization in Change Leadership. Richard is also a Certified Business Coaching Specialist and Certified Business Consultant with a green belt certification in Six Sigma, as well. He resides in Pittsburgh, PA.

Contact: RichardBell239@gmail.com